The
Distance
Between
Us
Young Readers
Edition

The Distance Between Us

Young Readers Edition

BY REYNA GRANDE

Modified for a Young Audience

ALADDIN

New York   London   Toronto   Sydney   New Delhi

ALADDIN

An imprint of Simon & Schuster Children's Publishing Division
1230 Avenue of the Americas, New York, New York 10020
First Aladdin hardcover edition September 2016
Text copyright © 2012, 2016 by Reyna Grande
Modified for a young audience
Jacket illustration copyright © 2016 by James Gulliver Hancock
Back cover photograph courtesy of author
Interior photographs courtesy of the author

For information about special discounts for bulk purchases, please contact
Simon & Schuster Special Sales at 1-866-506-1949 or business@simonandschuster.com.
The Simon & Schuster Speakers Bureau can bring authors to your live event. For more information
or to book an event, contact the Simon & Schuster Speakers Bureau at
1-866-248-3049 or visit our website at www.simonspeakers.com.
Jacket designed by Laura Lyn DiSiena
Interior designed by Steve Scott
The text of this book was set in ITC Cheltenham Light.
Manufactured in the United States of America 0617 FFG
4 6 8 10 9 7 5 3
Library of Congress Cataloging-in-Publication Data
Names: Grande, Reyna, author.
Title: The distance between us / by Reyna Grande.
Description: Young readers edition. | New York : Aladdin, Simon and Schuster Children's Publishing, [2016]
Identifiers: LCCN 2016024959 | ISBN 9781481463713 (hardcover)
Subjects: LCSH: Grande, Reyna—Childhood and youth—Juvenile literature. | Mexican Americans—Biography—
Juvenile literature. | Immigrants—United States—Biography—Juvenile literature. | Abused children—United
States—Biography—Juvenile literature. | Mexico—Emigration and immigration—Social aspects—Juvenile
literature. | United States—Emigration and immigration—Social aspects—Juvenile literature. | Mexican
Americans—California—Los Angeles—Biography—Juvenile literature. | Los Angeles (Calif.)—Biography—
Juvenile literature. | Mexican American women authors—Biography—Juvenile literature.
Classification: LCC E184.M5 G6652 2016 | DDC 305.8968/72073—dc23
LC record available at https://lccn.loc.gov/2016024959
ISBN 9781481463720 (eBook)

To my sister, Mago, my little mother

Dear Reader,

In recent years, more than 200,000 children have arrived at the U.S. border asking for permission to stay. Most are from countries such as Honduras, El Salvador, and Guatemala, and some from my own country—Mexico. They come escaping violence, poverty, persecution, corruption, but some also come to be reunited with their parents.

You see, in countries with extreme poverty and limited opportunities, many parents are forced to leave their children behind to go to a place where they can find a better life. Many of these children are left for years and years not knowing if they will ever see their parents again.

This is exactly what happened to me and my brother and sister. We were left in Mexico by both our mother and our father when they came to the U.S. to find better jobs. The years passed, and our desperation and fear grew. What if they forgot us? Or worse, what if they replaced us with American-born children? What if we never saw them again?

There were times when we thought about running away from our hometown to come and find our parents. We wanted to ask them, Do you still love us? Do you still want us? *Luckily, we never had to make that journey alone. My father did return for us eventually. And one day I found myself running across the U.S. border with my dad and two siblings, putting my life at risk to finally have the family I dreamed of.*

The immigrant children of today who have been arriving at the U.S. border have not had the same luck as me. They have been forced to flee their hometowns—often by themselves—to pursue their dream of having their parents by their side. Or worse, they come because their lives back home are in danger due to the instability and violence raging throughout Mexico and Central America.

I wrote The Distance Between Us *because I believe that immigrant children have important stories that need to be told. I thought that maybe if I told my story of being a child immigrant it would help shed light on the controversial issue of immigration. I hope that those who read my book would show compassion, understanding, and love toward all immigrants, especially child immigrants.*

This book was first published for adult readers, but I wanted to share my story with young readers as well, immigrant and nonimmigrant alike. Ultimately, The Distance Between Us *is about survival and triumph, of learning that no matter how difficult our childhoods might be, we owe it to ourselves to look toward the future with hope, and to not let anything or anyone keep us from becoming the kind of person we want to be.*

Where do you want to go? Who do you want to be? What do you want to achieve?

Hold on to your dreams, dear reader. When times get tough, hold on tight and don't let go.

Abrazos,
Reyna Grande

Part One

MI MAMÁ ME AMA

1

"I won't be gone long."

"How long?" I wanted to know. I needed to know.

"Not too long," Mami replied, closing her suitcase. She was going to a place most parents never come back from, a place that had already taken my father, and was now taking my mother.

The United States.

My sister, Mago; my brother, Carlos; and I grabbed our bags of clothes and followed Mami out the door of the little house we'd been renting. Mami's brothers were packing our belongings for storage. Just as we were about to step into the sunlight, I caught a glimpse of Papi. My uncle was putting a photo of my father into a box. I ran to take the photo from my uncle.

"Why are you taking that?" Mami said as we headed down the dirt road to Papi's mother's house, where we would be staying while Mami was gone.

"He's my papi," I said, and I clutched the frame tight against my chest.

"Your grandmother has pictures of him at her house," Mami said. "You don't need to take it with you."

"But *this* is my papi!" I said. She didn't understand that this paper face behind a wall of glass was the only father I knew.

Papi had left for the United States two years before. He wanted to build us a house—a real house made of brick and concrete. Even though he was a bricklayer and could build a house with his own hands, he couldn't find work in Mexico because of the weak economy, so he'd left to go to the place everyone in my hometown calls El Otro Lado, "The Other Side." Three weeks earlier he'd called Mami to tell her he needed her help. "If we're both here making dollars, it will be faster to buy the materials for the house," he'd said, then they would come back to Mexico to build our house.

But in the meantime he was leaving us without a mother.

Mago (short for Magloria) took my bag of clothes so I could hold Papi's photo with both hands. The dirt road was full of rocks waiting to trip me, but that day I was extra careful because I carried my papi in my arms, and he could break easily.

My hometown of Iguala de la Independencia in the southern state of Guerrero is surrounded by mountains. My grandmother lived on the edge of the city, and as we walked to her house, I kept my eyes on the closest mountain. It was big and smooth, as if covered by green velvet.

2

During the rainy season a circle of fog wrapped around its peak, like the white handkerchief people tie around their heads when they have headaches. This was why the locals had named it the Mountain That Has a Headache. Back then I didn't know what was on the other side, and Mami didn't either. She'd never been anywhere outside of Iguala. Until that day.

We didn't live far from Papi's mother, and as we turned the corner, her house came into view. Abuela Evila's house sat at the bottom of the hill. It was a small adobe house painted white with a terra-cotta tile roof. Bougainvillea climbed up on one side. The vine, thick with red flowers, made the house look as if it were bleeding.

"Listen to your grandmother," Mami said, startling me. All four of us had been quiet during our walk. She stopped and stood before us. "Behave yourselves. Don't give her any reason to get angry."

"She was born angry," Mago said under her breath.

Carlos and I giggled. Mami giggled too, but stopped. "Hush, Mago. Don't talk like that. Your abuela is doing us a favor by taking you in. Listen to her and always do as she says."

"But why do we have to stay with her?" Carlos asked. He'd be seven years old the following month. Mago was eight and a half years old, four years older than me.

"Why can't we stay with Abuelita Chinta?" Mago asked. I thought about Mami's mother. Her voice was soft like the cooing of the doves in the cages around her shack, and she smelled of almond oil and herbs. But as much as I loved my grandmother, I wanted my mother.

Mami sighed. "Your father wants you to stay with his mother. He thinks you'll be better off there—"

"But—"

"Basta. He has made a decision, and we must do as he says," Mami said.

We continued walking. Mago, Carlos, and I slowed down, and soon Mami was walking by herself. I looked at the photo in my arms, at Papi's black wavy hair, full lips, wide nose, and dark brown eyes looking to the left. I wished he was looking *at* me, and not past me. I wished he could *see* me.

"Why are you taking her away?" I asked the Man Behind the Glass. As always, he didn't answer me.

"Señora, we're here!" Mami shouted from the gate of my grandmother's house. From across the street the neighbor's dog barked at us.

"Señora, it's me, Juana!" Mami yelled, louder this time. She didn't open the gate to go in because my grandmother didn't like Mami. And the truth was my abuela Evila didn't like us, either, so I didn't understand why Papi wanted us to stay there.

Finally Abuela Evila came out of the house. Her silver hair was up in a bun so tight that it pulled her scalp. She walked bent to the ground, as if she were carrying an invisible sack of corn. As she came to the gate, she dried her hands on her apron, stained with fresh red sauce.

"We're here," Mami said.

"I see," my grandmother replied. She didn't open the gate, and she didn't ask us to come in and cool ourselves under the shade of the lemon tree in the patio. The bright noon sun burned my scalp. I got closer to Mami and hid in her shadow.

"Thank you for taking care of my children, señora," Mami said. "Every week we'll be sending you money for their upkeep."

My grandmother looked at the three of us. I couldn't tell if she was angry. She was always frowning, no matter what kind of mood she was in. "And how long will they be staying?"

"For as long as necessary," Mami said. "Only God knows how long it's going to take to build the house Natalio wants."

"*Natalio* wants?" Abuela Evila asked, leaning against the gate. "Don't you want it too?"

Mami looked at us and put her arms around us. We leaned against her. Tears stung my eyes, and I felt as if I'd swallowed one of Carlos's marbles.

"Of course, señora. What woman wouldn't want a nice brick house? But not at the price we must pay to have it," Mami said.

"American dollars go a long way here," Abuela Evila said, pointing at the brick house built on the far side of her property. "My daughter has built herself a very nice house with the money she's made in El Otro Lado."

5

We turned to look at the house. It was the biggest one on the block, but my aunt didn't live in it. She hadn't returned from the U.S. even though she'd left long before Papi had. She had left my cousin Élida behind, and my grandmother had been taking care of her since.

"I'm not talking about the money," Mami said to my grandmother. Then she turned to us and bent to be at eye level with us. She took a deep breath and said, "I'll work as hard as I can. Every dollar I earn will go to you and the house. We'll be back before you know it."

"Why did Papi only send for you and not me?" Mago asked. "I want to see him too." As the oldest, she remembered Papi better than I did. She longed for him more than I did.

"I told you why. Your father only had enough money for me. And I'm going there to work. To help him with the house."

"We don't need a house. We need Papi," Mago said.

"We need you," Carlos said.

Mami ran her fingers through Mago's hair. "I'll be gone a year. I promise by then I'll come back and bring your father with me. Do you promise to take care of Carlos and Reyna for me, be their little mother?"

Mago looked at Carlos, then at me. I didn't know what my sister saw in my eyes that made her face soften. Did she see how afraid I was? Did she see that my heart was breaking at losing my mother? "Sí, Mami. I promise. But you'll keep your promise, right? You will come back?"

6

"Of course," Mami said. She opened her arms to us, and we fell into them.

"Don't go, Mami. Stay with us. Stay with *me*. Please," I pleaded, holding on to her.

She kissed the top of my head and pushed me toward the closed gate. "You need to get out of the sun before it gives you a headache."

Abuela Evila finally opened the gate to allow us inside, but we didn't move. We stood there holding our bags, and I wanted to throw Papi's photo against the ground so it shattered into pieces. I hated him for taking my mother from me just because he wanted a house and a piece of land to call his own.

"Don't go, Mami. Please!" I begged.

Mami gave us each a hug and kissed us good-bye. I pressed my cheek against her lips painted red with Avon lipstick.

Mago held me tightly as we watched Mami walk away. When she disappeared where the road curved, I tore my hand from my sister's and took off running, yelling for my mother. Through my tears I watched a taxicab take her away. I felt a hand on my shoulder and turned to see Mago standing behind me.

"Come on, Nena," she said. There were no tears in her eyes, and as we walked back to my grandmother's house, I wondered if, when Mami had asked Mago to be our little mother, it had also meant she was not allowed to cry.

2

Every day, while Mago and Carlos were at school, I stood by the gate and looked down the dirt road where Mami had disappeared, hoping to see her return.

"Go inside, Nena," Mago said when she and Carlos arrived from school. She ushered me back into our grandmother's house, where we spent the rest of the afternoon doing nothing but chores.

"You won't stay here for free," Abuela Evila had said as soon as the gate had closed behind us that morning when Mami had left. And by now I knew she meant it.

Two weeks had gone by, and everyone in the neighborhood now knew our mother had left. We couldn't go anywhere without people looking at us with pity. One day Mago and I were passing by the baker's house on our way to the tortilla mill, and the baker's wife looked at us and said to her husband, "Look at them, poor little orphans."

"We aren't orphans!" I yelled. I grabbed a rock to throw at her, but I knew Mami would be disappointed in me if I threw it. So I let it fall to the ground.

8

Still, the baker's wife had seen the look in my eyes. She knew what I'd been about to do. "Shame on you, girl!" she scolded. "I would want the earth to swallow me whole if I had a daughter like you."

"Oh, don't be too harsh on the girl," the baker said. "It's a sad thing, not to have any parents." He got onto his bicycle to deliver his bread. I watched him until he turned the corner, mesmerized at how he wove his bike through the rocks on the dirt road without losing his balance and spilling all the bread in his giant hat basket.

"If your mother ever comes back, I'll be sure to tell her of your behavior," the baker's wife said, pointing a finger at me. She went into her house and slammed the door shut.

"I can't believe you," Mago said, whacking me with the straw tortilla basket.

My eyes stung with tears. "But we aren't orphans!"

She was too angry to speak to me. She held me tightly by the wrist and hurried me along to the tortilla mill. I stumbled on a rock and would have fallen if Mago hadn't been holding me. She slowed down and loosened her hold on my wrist.

"I don't want people feeling sorry for us," I told her.

She stopped walking then. She touched the scars on her face from an accident when she was little. There was a scar on her cheek, her eyelid, and on the bridge of her nose. People always felt sorry for Mago because of her scars, and she hated it.

"I'm sorry I hit you, Nena," she said. At hearing her call me *baby*, I immediately forgave her.

When we got back from the tortilla mill, my cousin Élida was waiting by the gate, asking why we'd taken so long. "Can't you see I'm hungry?" Élida, who was going on thirteen, had a round chubby face and big puffy eyes that looked like frog eyes. I thought that since we were all in the same situation—having been left behind by our parents—we would be friends. Élida wasn't interested in being our friend. Like the neighbors, she called us the little orphans, even though her mother had left her too. The pretty dresses Abuela Evila made for her on her sewing machine, and the many gifts her mother sent her from El Otro Lado, helped Élida transform herself from the little orphan to a privileged granddaughter. She was everything we were not.

At seeing her, I got angry again at being called an orphan, at being hit by Mago, at my mother for leaving me, at my father for taking her away. "Your hair looks like a horse's tail," I said.

"Stupid orphan!" she said, yanking my pigtail. Abuela Evila took the tortillas from Mago and didn't say anything to Élida for pulling my hair.

Carlos, Mago, and I sat on the two concrete steps leading from the kitchen to my grandmother's bedroom, since the table was only big enough for four people, and those seats were already taken. Abuela Evila gave a pork chop to my grandfather. Another to Élida. The third to my aunt, Tía Emperatriz, and the last pork chop she took for herself. By the time the frying pan came our way, there was nothing but oil left. Abuela Evila scooped up spoonfuls of oil and mixed it in with our beans. "For flavor," she said.

If Papi were here, if Mami were here, we wouldn't be eating oil, I thought.

"Isn't there any meat left?" Tía Emperatriz asked.

Abuela Evila shook her head. "The money you left me this morning didn't go very far at el mercado," she said. "And their parents haven't sent me anything this week."

My aunt looked at our oily beans. She grabbed her purse and gave Mago a coin to buy us a soda. Mago came back from the store with a Fanta. We thanked our aunt and took turns sipping from the bottle, but the sweet taste of orange didn't wash away the oil in our mouths.

"What's the point of them being in El Otro Lado if we're going to be eating like beggars?" Mago said after our meal. We took the dirty dishes out to the washing stone. Then we cleaned the table and swept the dirt floor. Carlos took the trash can out to the backyard to burn the pile of garbage.

"Regina!" Abuela Evila called out from her bedroom, where she was mending her dresses. "Regina, come here!" she said. It took me a moment to realize she was calling me, since Regina isn't my name. But I was born on September 7, the day of Saint Regina, and my grandmother chose that

11

name for me at my birth. Mami disobeyed her and named me Reyna instead.

"Yes, Abuela?" I said as I came to the door.

"Go to Don Bartolo's store to buy me a needle," she said, handing me a coin. "And hurry back."

Don Bartolo's two daughters were playing hopscotch outside his store. When they saw me walking past them, they pointed at me and said, "Look, there goes the little orphan." This time I didn't think twice. I didn't care if the whole neighborhood thought I was wild and a disgrace to my family. I threw the coin as hard as I could. It hit the taller girl above her right eye. She screamed and ran into the store, calling to her father. I ran home as fast as I could, leaving the coin on the ground. When Abuela Evila asked me for her needle, I had no choice but to tell her the truth.

She called Mago over and said, "Take your sister to apologize to Don Bartolo, and don't come back without my needle."

Mago grabbed my hand and pulled me along. "Now you've done it," she said.

"She shouldn't have called me an orphan!" I yanked my hand from Mago's and stopped walking. She looked at me for a long time. I thought she was going to hit me, but instead she took my hand and pulled me along in the other direction.

"Where are we going?" I asked. She didn't tell me

where she was taking me, but as soon as we turned the corner, the little house we had once rented came into view. We stopped in front of it. The window was open, and I could smell beans boiling on the stove. I heard the sound of a woman singing along to the radio. Mago said she didn't know who the new tenants were, but it'd always be the house where we'd lived with our parents. "No one can take that away," she said. "I know you don't remember Papi at all, but whatever you remember about Mami and this house is yours to keep forever."

I followed her down to the canal at the bottom of the hill. Mami would do the washing here. "This is where Mami saved your life, Nena. Remember?" Mago said.

I nodded, feeling a lump in my throat. The year before, I'd almost drowned in the canal. The rainy season had turned it into a gushing river, and the current had been swift and strong. Mami had told me to sit on the washing stones and stay by her side, but she'd let Mago and Carlos get into the water and play with the other kids. I wanted to get in, and when Mami was busy rinsing our clothes and looking the other way, I jumped in. The current pulled me down the canal. I couldn't touch the bottom. Mami got to me just in time.

Now we went back to Abuela Evila's house, not knowing what we were going to tell her. Before we went into the house itself, Mago took me into the small shack of bamboo sticks and cardboard near the patio. Inside were large clay pots, a big griddle, and other pots and pans. I'd been born in this shack. This was where Mami and Papi had first lived when they'd gotten married.

Mago and I sat on the dirt floor, and she told me about the day I was born, exactly the way Mami used to tell it. She pointed to the circle of rocks and a pile of ash and told me that during my birth a fire had been burning. When I was born, the midwife put me into my mother's arms, and Mami turned to face the fire to keep me warm. As I listened to Mago now, I closed my eyes and felt the heat of the flames and heard Mami's heart beating against my ear.

Mago pointed to a spot on the dirt floor and reminded me that my umbilical cord was buried there. *That way,* Mami had told the midwife, *no matter where life takes her, she won't ever forget where she came from.*

But then Mago touched my belly button and said something my mother had never said. She said my umbilical cord was like a ribbon that connected me to Mami. She said, "It doesn't matter that there's a distance between us now. That cord is there forever." I touched my belly button, and I thought about what my sister had said. I had Papi's photo to keep me connected to him. I had no photo of my mother, but now my sister had given me something to remember her by.

"We still have a mother and a father," Mago said. "We aren't orphans, Nena. Just because they aren't with us doesn't mean we don't have parents anymore. Now come on. Let's go tell our grandmother we have no needle for her."

"She's going to beat me," I said as we headed to the

14

house. "And she's going to beat you, too, even though you didn't do anything."

"I know," she said.

"Wait," I said. I ran out of the gate before I lost my nerve. I ran down the street as fast as I could. Outside the store Don Bartolo's daughters were playing again. They glared at me the moment they saw me. Suddenly my feet didn't want to keep walking. I put a finger on my belly button.

"I'm sorry I hit you with the coin," I told the girl.

She turned to look at her father, who came out to stand by the door. She said, "My papi says we're lucky he has the store. If he didn't, he would have to leave for El Otro Lado. I wouldn't want him to go."

"I didn't want Mami to go either," I said. "But she'll be back soon. And so will my papi."

Don Bartolo took my grandmother's coin from his pocket and handed it to me. "Don't ever think that your parents don't love you," he said. "It is because they love you very much that they have left."

I bought the needle for Abuela Evila, and as I walked home, I told myself maybe Don Bartolo was right. I had to keep on believing that my parents had left me because they loved me too much, and not because they didn't love me enough.

3

It didn't take long for Élida and us to become bitter ene-
mies. She was the favored grandchild, and she always
made sure we didn't forget it. When she had arrived
at Abuela Evila's house six years before, when she was
seven, my grandmother had kicked my grandfather out of
her bed to make space for Élida in her bedroom. Anything
Élida wanted, she would get—a new dress, a new pair of
shoes, treats, and unlimited time watching television. At
my grandmother's insistence Élida's mother would send
her presents too. Once, she got a Walkman from El Otro
Lado, and she was the envy of the whole neighborhood. At
home she would spend hours lying on the hammock listening to Michael Jackson songs on her Walkman while
we three cleaned the house from top to bottom.

Another time my grandmother thought Élida
should learn how to type so she could be the best secretary Iguala had ever had, and soon after a typewriter
arrived from El Otro Lado. Élida would spend hours
tap-tap-tapping away while we three did nothing but

chores and longed for our own presents from El Otro Lado.

She hardly ever shared her stuff with us, and whenever she allowed us to play with her dolls, we had to play the role of the maids and she was always the rich woman. She was even bossier than my grandmother! Then we didn't want to play anymore because it was bad enough being bossed around in real life, let alone when we were supposed to be playing.

But the worst thing about Élida was the nicknames she had given us. She called me Chueca, "crooked," because I am left-handed, so she said I was deformed. Carlos she called Calaca, "skeleton," because he was extremely skinny, except for his big belly full of tapeworm. And Mago's nickname was Piojosa, because of all the lice she had on her head. Carlos and I tolerated the nicknames as much as we could, but not Mago. She and Élida were constantly fighting like old ladies, and things went from bad to worse the day Mago threatened to infest Élida's hair with lice.

Élida's hair was her most prized possession. It was so long that it tumbled down her back like a sparkling black waterfall. Every few days Abuela Evila washed Élida's hair with lemon water to keep it shiny and healthy. In the afternoons Abuela Evila would fill up a bucket from the water tank, cut lemons off the tree, and squeeze the juice into the water.

17

Mago, Carlos, and I would hide behind a bush and watch through the leaves. Abuela Evila washed Élida's hair as if it were an expensive and delicate silk shawl. Afterward Élida would sit under the sun to dry her hair. My grandmother then brushed it in small strokes, beginning with the tips and working her way up. She spent half an hour running the comb through Élida's long, long hair while we watched.

Our hair was full of lice, our bellies swollen with tapeworm, but my grandmother didn't care. She said, "Maybe you aren't even my grandchildren."

Sometimes I wished she was right. I didn't want her to be my grandmother either.

"Your mother is not coming back for you," Élida said to us one afternoon while lying in the sun to let her hair dry. "Now that she's got a job and is making dollars, she won't want to come back, believe me."

Three weeks before, Mami had called us on the phone and told us she'd gotten a job at a garment factory. She'd said she was finally helping Papi save money for the house, and had promised to send us money for shoes and clothes. We couldn't tell Mami not to bother, that the money they sent disappeared by the time my grandmother made it home from the bank. My grandmother would stand next to us while we talked on the phone, and if we said anything bad about her, she would spank us.

"She'll be back. I know she will," Mago told Élida. In the two and a half months we'd been there, my parents

18

had called us every other weekend. Mago would remind Mami of her promise—that she would return in a year.

"Don't lie to yourself," Élida said. "They're going to forget all about you, you'll see. You're always going to be the little orphans."

"Speak for yourself. It's your mother who's not coming back," Mago said. "Doesn't she have another child over there in El Otro Lado?"

At being reminded of her American brother, Élida looked away. Abuela Evila came out of the house carrying a large plastic comb. She sat behind Élida and combed her long hair that smelled of lemonade. Élida was quiet, and she didn't answer Abuela Evila when she asked her what was wrong.

An hour later Élida was back on the patio. She lay down on the hammock and watched us do our chores. Mago swept while I watered Abuela Evila's pots of vinca and geraniums. Carlos was in the backyard helping my grandfather clear the brush.

Élida rocked herself in the hammock, eating a mango-on-a-stick that she'd bought at Don Bartolo's store. It was a beautiful mango cut to look like a rose, its yellow flesh sprinkled with red chili powder. My mouth watered at seeing her take a bite.

"My mother loves me," she said.

"Oh, shut up already," Mago said. She turned the broom to face Élida and swept toward her.

19

"Stupid orphan!" Élida yelled, scrambling to get away from the cloud of dust Mago had sent her way. "Piojosa!"

"So what if I have lice?" Mago said. "And if you aren't careful, I'll give them to you, and we'll see what happens to all that pretty hair of yours." Mago pulled me to her and started parting my hair. "Look, look, a louse!" she said, holding it out to Élida.

"Abuelita! Abuelita!" Élida yelled, her eyes opened wide with fear. She ran into the house holding on to her thick long braid. Mago and I looked at each other.

"Look what you've done. We're really going to get it now," I said to Mago.

I thought we were going to get a beating with my grandmother's wooden spoon, or a branch or a sandal, the usual choices. I would have preferred a beating to what we got.

In the evening, when my aunt came home from work, Abuela Evila told her to take care of our lice problem. My aunt gave Mago money and sent her to buy kerosene, a really smelly oil used to light lamps—and kill lice. The last rays of the sun were gone, and darkness fell around us. My grandmother turned on the light on the patio, but it didn't work. There was no power that night. She brought out her candles and set them on the water tank.

When Mago returned with the kerosene, my aunt sat us down one by one.

"What if that doesn't work?" Élida asked.

"If the kerosene doesn't work, I'm shaving off their hair!" Abuela Evila said.

At hearing my grandmother's words, I stopped squirming. Tía Emperatriz ran through my hair with a lice comb. She made me tilt my head all the way back and poured kerosene onto my hair. The smell made my head spin. She made sure every strand of hair was covered before wrapping my head with a towel and tying a plastic bag over it to keep it in place. I sat so still, I could hear the mosquitoes buzzing around. They bit my legs and arms, but the thought of getting my head shaved kept me from moving.

"Now off to bed," my aunt said when she was done, "but stay away from the lit candles."

My grandmother had given us a twin-size bed for the three of us to share. It was tucked into a corner of my grandfather's room. I slept in the middle between Mago and Carlos so that I wouldn't fall off. We would huddle together at night, clinging to each other, even though Carlos had started wetting the bed soon after Mami had left.

But that night I wasn't worried about being peed on. It was a long, restless night, and we couldn't sleep! I wanted to scratch, scratch, scratch, but I couldn't. The overwhelming smell of the kerosene made me dizzy. I tried to hold my breath for as long as I could, and when my lungs were bursting, I would take in a big gulp of air and feel my head spinning like a top. I reached for my towel and pulled on it, not able to bear the pain any longer.

"Leave it alone," Mago said.

"It hurts so much," I said. "I need to scratch. I really need to."

"My scalp feels as if it's on fire!" Carlos said. "I can't take it anymore."

"Don't do it," Mago said. "We'll get our hair chopped off if you ruin it now."

"I don't care!" With one swoop of his hand, Carlos pulled off the towel.

A half hour later I did the same.

Abuela Evila was true to her word. The next afternoon, when my grandfather came home from work, she had him take out his razor blade and scissors. Carlos's hair was completely shaved off. We ran our hands over his bald head, feeling the stubble tickle our palms. When she saw him, Élida burst out laughing. "Now you really do look like a skeleton." She started to sing a song. "*La calaca, tilica y flaca. La calaca, tilica y flaca.*" I laughed because it was a funny song and I could picture the lank and skinny skeleton dancing along to it.

"Regina, it's your turn," Abuela Evila said.

"Please, Abuelita, no!" I yelled as my grandmother dragged me to the chair. My grandfather hit me on the head with his hand and ordered me to sit still.

"It's up to you if you want to move," he said when I wouldn't stop. "Just don't blame me for how the haircut turns out."

I jerked around, crying and yelling for Mami to come. I hated myself for being so weak the night before, when I'd torn the towel off. Tears rolled down my face, and I cried for my hair, because I loved my hair. It was the only beautiful thing I had, curls so thick that women in the street would stop and touch them and tell Mami "What lovely hair your daughter has. She looks like a doll," and Mami would smile with pride.

"Don't move, Nena. He's doing a really bad job!" Mago said. But I didn't listen, and the scissors hissed near my ear. I squirmed even more at watching my curls spill onto the ground and onto my lap, falling one by one like flower petals. Then my grandmother's chickens came clucking to see what was happening. They picked up my curls and shook them around. They stepped all over them and dragged them with their feet across the dirt.

In the end, when Abuelo Augurio was done, I ran to the mirror. My hair was as short as a boy's, and it was so uneven, it looked as if a cow had nibbled on it! I hid under my covers and didn't come out. I looked at Papi's photo hanging on the wall. I'd looked at myself in the mirror enough times to know that his slanted eyes were just like mine. We both had small foreheads, wide cheeks, and a wide nose. And now we both had short, black hair.

"When are you coming back?" I asked the Man Behind the Glass. "Do you love me?"

I wished I had a picture of Mami. I wanted to tell her I missed being with her. I missed going to the canal and sitting on the washing stone while she scrubbed our clothes and told me stories. If the water was low, she would let me get in and chase after the soap bubbles as she dunked the clothes into the water to rinse.

I missed going with her to visit Abuelita Chinta and taking a nap on my grandmother's bed while they talked. I would fall asleep listening to Mami's voice and the cooing of my grandmother's doves. And at night I missed snuggling with her on the bed she'd shared with Papi. Mago and I would try to keep Mami warm so she wouldn't miss him so much.

Mago came in to tell me it was dinnertime. I looked at her and hated her because she hadn't gotten her hair chopped off. She'd dealt with the stupid scratching all night long, and in the morning she'd woken up and the lice had all been dead. Even though she'd washed her hair twenty times with Tía Emperatriz's shampoo that smelled of roses, it still reeked of kerosene. But at least she didn't look like a boy.

"Leave me alone," I said.

"Come on, Nena. Come and eat."

My stomach didn't care that my hair had been butchered. It groaned with hunger, and I had no choice but to go out into the kitchen, where everyone could see me. Tía

Emperatriz, who'd been at work when the hair cutting had taken place, gasped at seeing me and said, "Ay, Amá, what did you do to this poor girl?"

Élida said, "What girl? Isn't that Carlos?" When I glared at her, she laughed and said, "Oops, I thought you were your brother."

That night I had a dream about Mami. In my dream she was washing my still-long black hair with lemon water and scrubbing it so gently that I sighed with pleasure. I woke up with a pain in my heart, and I felt like crying. Then I realized that Carlos had wet our bed and I was soaked.

4

We'd been at Abuela Evila's house for six months, and it was worse than a prison. We weren't allowed to go out except to run errands. My grandmother didn't let us play with the neighborhood kids because she said she was responsible for us and didn't want us getting into trouble. But on Saturday mornings she and Élida would go downtown, and we would sneak out of the house and rush to the vacant lot. There was an abandoned car there where we liked to play. The car was rusty and the seats were full of holes. It had no tires, but the steering wheel worked just fine.

"Where are we off to today?" Carlos asked, taking his turn at the wheel.

"To El Otro Lado," I said.

"Vroom. Vroom! Here we go," Carlos said.

The noises got louder. The car went faster. Carlos said, "Hold on tight for the jump! Yeee-haa!" As he drove, I looked at the Mountain That Has a Headache and was sure El Otro Lado was over there. Mago said the United

States was really far away, and what could be farther away than an unknown town on the other side of the mountains?

"Head that way," I told Carlos as I pointed to the mountain. "That's where Mami and Papi are."

Carlos started the noises again. The engine revved, and soon we were off. "Yeee-haa!"

Since I decided my parents were on the other side of the Mountain That Has a Headache, I would look at the mountain every night and wish them a buenas noches. In the morning I wished them a buenos días. Carlos and Mago did it too, even though Élida laughed and said we were a bunch of idiots to believe our parents were that close to us.

"My mami and papi are as close as I want them to be," I said to Élida.

At first I didn't really know where to find Papi. All I had was his photo. But one day, as we were walking to the store, Mago stopped outside a house to listen to "Escuché Las Golondrinas" playing on the radio and said, "Papi loved that song." That was how I learned to find Papi in the voice of Vicente Fernández. Another time, as we were walking to the tortilla mill, the mail carrier passed by on his bicycle, and we caught a whiff of something spicy, like cinnamon, and Mago said, "That's how Papi smelled!" I learned to find him in a bottle of Old Spice we found in a trash heap.

27

It was easier to find Mami. She was in the smell of the apple-scented shampoo my aunt bought for us. She was in the scent of her favorite Avon perfumes I smelled on her old friends when I stood in line with them at the tortilla mill. I found the color of her lips in the flowers of the bougainvillea climbing up Abuela Evila's house. I heard Mami in the lyrics of her favorite songs from Los Dandys. And when Abuelita Chinta came to visit us, I saw Mami in her mother's eyes.

Never a day went by when I didn't go into the little shack where I'd been born. I traced a circle around the spot where my umbilical cord had been buried, and thought about the special cord that connected me to Mami.

Every two weeks when they called, I would find my parents in my grandmother's phone. But always those precious two minutes when Abuela Evila allowed us to talk would go by too quickly. Two minutes to tell them everything we felt. So many things to say to them, but one night in August we said nothing at all. It was Mami who talked, who gave us the worst news of all.

She was going to have a baby.

"They're replacing us already," Mago said after handing the phone back to Abuela Evila. We went to the room we shared with our grandfather, and since there was no door, only a thin curtain, we could hear our grandmother telling my parents how tough things were and could they please send more money? "Your children need shoes and clothes . . . ," Abuelita Evila said. But last time, when

28

they'd sent the money she asked for, she'd used it to make Élida a new dress.

"They'll leave us here and forget all about us," Mago said. Carlos and I tried to make her feel better, but it was no use. I held my sister and cried with her. I felt so angry at my parents. I couldn't understand why they'd asked God for another child. *Aren't we three enough?* I put a finger on my belly button and thought of the cord that tied me to Mami. As long as that cord existed, she wouldn't forget me, no matter how many other children she had. But Papi, what connected me to him? What would keep him from forgetting me?

The day after the telephone call, Mago refused to go to school, and Carlos had to walk alone. Mago spent all day in our room. She grabbed a history book and flipped through the pages until she found a map. She traced a line between two dots, and because I couldn't yet read, I didn't know what the letters spelled. "What are you doing?" I asked.

She showed me the map. "This is Iguala. And this is Los Angeles, and this," she said as she made her finger go from one dot to the other, "this is the distance between us and our parents."

I touched my belly button and said, "But we're connected."

She shrugged and said, "I just made that up to make you feel better."

"You're lying!" I said. I kicked her on the calf and ran out of the room with a finger on my belly button. I hid in the shack where I'd been born and cried myself to sleep.

I awoke to the sound of someone shouting my grandmother's name at the gate, and I went out to see that Doña Paula had arrived. Since we lived on the outskirts of Iguala, we didn't have running water. Doña Paula came every three days to deliver water from the community well. Her donkey carried two large water containers on either side. Her two boys rode on the donkey while she walked alongside it, pulling on the reins.

"Buenas tardes," she said to Abuela Evila as she led the donkey through the gate.

As always she kissed each of her sons on the mouth as she helped them get off the donkey one by one. We had no mother to give us kisses anymore. And now our mother would have a brand-new baby to kiss.

"Look at those mama's boys," Mago said from behind me. "What a bunch of sissies." When their mother wasn't looking, I stuck out my tongue at them.

Doña Paula told her sons to go play with us while she visited with my grandmother. We loved playing in the backyard, but Mago didn't want to play with Doña Paula's sons that day. So they went off on their own, and we went to the north side of the house, where the alley was. By the rock fence encircling Abuela's property was a big pile of human poop.

Mago yanked my arm and said, "Nena, go get me two tortillas."

"What for?"

"Just do it, and heat them up too. We don't want them cold."

I snuck into the kitchen, being careful not to be caught by my grandmother and Doña Paula. *What is Mago up to?* I ran back and gave her the tortillas. She jumped over the fence, scooped up some poop with a stick, and buttered the tortillas with it. Then she rolled them up and went to find Doña Paula's boys.

"You boys hungry?" she asked.

"We don't want any," they said, eyeing the tacos with distrust.

She held her hand up and curled it into a fist. "If you don't eat them, I'm going to beat you up," she said. "I mean it."

"Mago, stop it," I said. "Please!" But Mago pushed me away, and I wanted to cry because I didn't recognize my sister. It wasn't the boys' fault that Mami had given us the worst news ever. It wasn't their fault they still had a mother and ours was far, far away.

I watched in horror when the boys took a bite out of the tacos. Their eyes widened with disgust as they chewed and then spat onto the ground. "What's in them?"

"They're just bean tacos," Mago said.

"We don't want them," they said, running back to their mother.

"I can't believe you, Mago!" I said. We watched Doña Paula do her usual routine—first she picked up one boy, kissed him on the mouth, and put him on the donkey. She picked up the smaller boy. But this time when she kissed him, she made a face. She sniffed and sniffed and then wiped something off the corner of his mouth.

"You smell like caca, mijo," she said. She sniffed some more and said, "It *is* caca. Why do you have it on your mouth?" The little boy pointed at us and told her we'd given them bean tacos. "You little witches, why did you feed poop to my sons?"

We didn't wait to hear what Abuela Evila said. We raced to the backyard and climbed up a tree and didn't come down when our grandmother called us. She stood below us, waving a branch. "You better get down right now!" But we didn't. She finally tired of yelling and went back into the house. "You'll come down soon enough when you're hungry," she said.

We were there for so long that Élida and Carlos came home from school. Carlos couldn't get us to come down either, so he climbed up the tree and sat with us, and we told him what we'd done. "People call us little orphans because that's what we are, don't you see?" Mago said.

Carlos tried to make Mago laugh by telling us his favorite jokes of a boy named Pepito. "Shut up," she said. The sun went down, and soon the fireflies were out and about. Mosquitoes buzzed around and bit us. Our butts were sore from sitting on the hard tree branch. From up there we saw Tía Emperatriz come home.

"Ay Dios mio, niños, what are you doing up there in that tree at this hour?"

We came down and told her what we had done. She tried to stop Abuela Evila from giving us a beating but didn't succeed. My grandmother hit us one by one, beginning with Mago because she'd been the instigator. Mago bit her lips and didn't cry when the branch whistled through the air and hit her on the legs, back, and arms. Carlos did cry, first because he hadn't done anything and second out of humiliation because Abuela Evila made him pull down his pants, saying if she hit him with his pants on, he wouldn't learn his lesson. I wailed like La Llorona, the wailing woman herself, and called out for my missing mother.

5

In September I turned five, and Mago turned nine soon after. One Saturday morning my grandmother reluctantly handed Tía Emperatriz the money my parents had sent for a birthday cake. This was the third birthday I celebrated without Papi. The first without Mami.

The cake was beautiful. It was white and had pink sugar flowers all over. My aunt took pictures of us cutting the cake to send to our parents. We rarely had our pictures taken. The thought of the photos making their way to El Otro Lado—to Papi and Mami—was very exciting. I hoped those pictures would remind them of us so they wouldn't forget they still had three children waiting for them to return.

I smiled the biggest smile I could manage, to show I appreciated the money they'd sent for the cake. Carlos smiled halfway. He was very self-conscious about his crooked teeth. Mago didn't smile. She said that if she looked sad, then maybe our parents would see how much she truly missed them, and they'd come back.

From that point on she looked sad in almost every picture we took.

Her tactic didn't work. The pictures were sent, the months went by, and still our parents did not return.

The one who did return was Élida's mother. We had been at Abuela Evila's house for a little more than a year when Élida turned fifteen. She officially became a señorita, a little woman, and her mother came to Iguala to throw a big Quinceañera for her, to celebrate such an important moment in her daughter's life. A Quinceañera was every girl's dream, a party where you got to wear a beautiful princess dress and dance a waltz while everyone watched you twirl across the floor, and they clapped for you for becoming a young woman. My aunt arrived loaded with so many suitcases that she hired two taxis to take her from the bus station to Abuela Evila's house. While everyone greeted her and made a big fuss about her visit, we hid in a corner of the living room, eyeing the suitcases, wondering if our parents had sent us anything.

Élida's little brother, Javier, was six years old. He held on to Tía María Félix, and when Élida tried to hug my aunt, Javier pushed Élida away. "No, she's my mommy."

Abuela Evila scolded him. "She's Élida's mother too." But he wouldn't let go of his mom.

Then my aunt looked at us and gave us the worst news of all. "Your mother just had a little girl," she said. "Elizabeth, I think is what your mom named her."

35

With a heavy heart we went to our grandfather's room and lay on our bed.

"A baby girl," Mago said, breaking the silence. Yes, a girl, just like me and her. What did Carlos have to worry about? He was still the only boy. But us? What chance did we have now of our parents loving us, if they had a new little girl? A baby born in the United States. And it suddenly hit me: I was no longer the youngest. Some other girl I did not know had replaced me.

The next day all my cousins showed up to see what Tía María Félix had brought for them from El Otro Lado. We watched as she gave our cousins presents—a shirt, a pair of shoes, a toy. We waited our turn, and when the suitcases were empty, Tía María Félix turned to us with a sad look on her face and said, "Your parents sent you something, but unfortunately I lost that suitcase at the airport. . . ."

"That's a lie," Mago said. "Those toys that you gave away were for us! I know it. I just know it."

"You insolent child," Abuela Evila said. "I'm going to teach you to respect your elders." By the time she'd unbuckled the strap of her sandal, the three of us had already bolted out the door and headed to the backyard to climb up the trees.

"She could have given us something from the stuff she brought. It's not our fault she lost the suitcase," Carlos said.

"Don't be an idiot," Mago said, punching him on the arm. She jumped off the branch, climbed over the fence, and disappeared down the dirt road leading to the house where we used to live.

On the day of the party, everyone fussed over Élida. A hairstylist did her hair up in tiny braids held together by pink-and-white bows. Her mother, our grandmother, and Tía Emperatriz helped her put on the crinoline, the girdle, and the beautiful pink dress made with yards and yards of satin and tulle. I hated seeing Tía Emperatriz fussing over Élida so much. Usually she didn't pay much attention to her, but she was always nice to us.

While everyone went to church for the ceremony, we spent the morning plucking chickens. By the time we'd finished, the whole patio was covered in feathers, some floating in the air like white flower petals. Afterward, even though we took a bath and scrubbed ourselves with apple-scented shampoo, we still smelled like wet chicken feathers, and once in a while throughout the evening we pulled out feathers buried in our hair. I pretended I was turning into a dove. I imagined flying in search of my parents.

The Quinceañera was held at a beautiful reception hall. Élida looked like a princess, wearing her puffy pink dress and matching slippers. Mago spent the whole time sitting in a corner of the hall, feeling sorry for herself and jealous of Élida. "That stupid frog eyes doesn't deserve this stupid party."

Carlos took advantage of the fact that everyone was too busy to see him sneaking into the kitchen to stuff himself as much as he wanted. I spent the whole time hiding under a table, crying about the fact that my parents had replaced me.

I only came out to see the waltz, the highlight of any Quinceañera party. Élida danced with her escort, and then she danced with the godparents. The last waltz was meant to be danced with her father, as is tradition, but since her father wasn't there, she danced that waltz with my aunt's cousin, who was a butcher. He raised and killed pigs and had a restaurant where he sold posole, chorizo, chicharrón, and everything else that comes from pigs. "Look at her, dancing with the pig man," Mago said. "How appropriate."

My eyes watered as I watched Élida dance with a man that wasn't her father. I prayed for Papi to come back soon. When I turned fifteen, I didn't want to dance the waltz with anyone but him.

As Tía María Félix was packing and getting ready to go back to the United States, Carlos said, "Tía, what does El Otro Lado look like?" He wanted to know more about the place where our parents lived.

"El Otro Lado is a beautiful place," my aunt said. "Every street is paved with concrete. You don't see any dirt roads there. There's no trash in the streets like here. There are trucks that pick up the trash every week.

And you know what the best thing is? The trees there are special—they grow money. They have dollar bills for leaves."

She took some green bills out of her purse and showed them to us. "These are dollars," she said. We'd never seen dollars, but they were as green as the leaves on the trees we liked to climb. "Now picture a tree covered in dollar bills!"

She left in the afternoon with little Javier, promising Élida that one day soon she would send for her. For now Élida had to stay behind and watch a taxicab take her mother away. Abuela Evila put her arm around Élida and held her while she cried. It was so strange to see my cousin's face bathed in tears. Her mocking gaze was gone. The Élida who made fun of us, who laughed at us, who called us little orphans, had been replaced by a weeping, lonely, heartbroken girl.

Mago grabbed our hands and took us to the backyard to give Élida privacy. "I love you both," she said, and pulled us close to her. I realized then how lucky Mago, Carlos, and I were. We at least had each other. Élida was on her own.

We talked about those special dollar trees. Even though we knew that what my aunt had said couldn't be true, we fantasized about those trees anyway.

"If we had trees like that here, Papi wouldn't have had to leave," I said. "He could have bought the brick and cement and built us a house with his own hands."

We talked about the day when our parents would return. Carlos's fantasy was that they would fly to us in their own private helicopter. "I can just picture it," he said. "It would land here, in the middle of the yard." We giggled at the image of Papi emerging from the helicopter, his hair blowing in the wind, his face framed by aviator sunglasses, and Mami standing next to him, looking just as glamorous. We pictured the whole neighborhood rushing over to see them come home. And we would be so proud.

6

After feeling like a prisoner at my grandmother's house, finally my first day of first grade had arrived, and with that—freedom! Or so I thought. I'd been waiting for this day for a long time. Abuela Evila hadn't sent me to kindergarten, but finally I was in school, and I would get to be out of the house for several hours, out of my grandmother's sight. Best of all I would get my own books, like the ones Mago and Carlos brought home, books full of beautiful poetry and fun stories with colorful pictures of clouds, stars, people, and animals, like foxes and birds. I liked it when Mago read to me from her books, but I wanted to learn to read them myself.

At eight a.m. sharp Carlos, Mago, and I lined up with the rest of the students around the school's courtyard to salute the flag.

The color guard marched around the courtyard. When the flag passed by me, I stood straighter and kept my hand firmly pressed against my chest in salutation as I sang the national anthem.

Mago had told me we should be proud to be from Iguala because it was there, in that city, where the treaty that ended the Mexican War of Independence had been written. It was there, in Iguala, where the first Mexican flag had been made on February 24, 1821. This is why Iguala is called Cuna de la Bandera Nacional, "Birthplace of the National Flag." The first time the national anthem was sung, it was there, in Iguala.

I looked at the flag with new eyes, a newfound admiration, and as I sang, I puffed out my chest, feeling especially proud about having being born in Iguala de la Independencia.

My school was small. It was shaped like a square, with all the classrooms facing the courtyard. It had two bathrooms, one for boys and one for girls, but no running water. We had to fill up a bucket from the water tank inside and dump it into the toilet. But at least there was a toilet. We didn't have one at home.

When the morning activities were over, we lined up, and our teachers led us into our classrooms. We took our seats, and after a brief introduction el maestro started our lesson by teaching us the alphabet. He said we should have learned it in kindergarten, but half the students in the class hadn't gone to kindergarten. We repeated after him, and I was proud to already know my letters because Mago had taught them to me. When he told us to write our names down, I didn't have to look at the board to spell my name: *R-E-Y-N—*

I felt a stinging on my hand, and it took me a second to realize that el maestro had hit me with his ruler. "What are you doing?" he asked. He held his ruler in his right hand and tapped it over and over on the palm of his left hand.

"I'm writing my name," I said. "See?" I lifted my brand-new notebook to show him. I hoped he'd notice the pretty curly tail on the *Y*, like Mago had shown me how to do.

"You're not to write with that hand," he said. He took the pencil from my left hand and made me hold it with my right. "If I see you using your left hand, I will have to hit you again. Understood?"

My eyes stung with tears because the students had stopped their work to look at me. I took a deep breath and nodded. He walked away, and I looked down at the notebook. I wrote and erased, wrote and erased, and no matter how hard I tried, the letters didn't come out right. It was like trying to write with my feet!

Abuela Evila and Élida always teased me for being left-handed. My mother's father had also been left-handed. Since he'd died a week before I was born, Mami said he had given this gift to me. And that was how I had always seen it, as a gift from my grandfather, up until we came to Abuela Evila's house. She didn't agree. She said the left hand was the hand of the devil and I was evil for using it. Sometimes during meals she hit my hand with a wooden spoon and told me to eat with my right hand.

"Don't you know the right side is the side of God?" she

43

asked. "The left side is the side of the devil. You don't want to be evil, do you?" Since I didn't want anything to do with the devil, I picked up my spoon with my right hand and tried to eat with it. But I could only manage a few bites before my spoon found its way back to my left hand.

Just like my grandmother, just like Élida, who called me Crooked, my teacher made me feel ashamed about my left hand. He didn't understand that my pencil obeyed my left hand but not the right one. I tried once again to write my name, but the letters came out all twisted and ugly, and I found myself hating my name, hating my teacher, and hating school.

I met Mago and Carlos during recess by the jacaranda tree in the courtyard. By the entrance of the school, women were selling food. They had baskets filled with enchiladas, taquitos, and picaditas. The smell of the chile guajillo sauce, fresh cheese, and onion wafted toward us, and I asked them why we weren't getting in line to buy food.

Mago laughed.

"Our grandmother never gives us lunch money," Carlos said. "You better get used to it."

We watched the women put the food onto paper plates and hand them to the students who had brought money. We weren't the only ones drooling over the food. At least half of the children in the school were leaning against classroom walls, grabbing their empty bellies while staring at the food stands.

I looked at the glass containers of agua fresca at the food stand, drinks made out of cantaloupe, watermelon, and pineapple. I could see the large cubes of ice swimming inside the glass containers. My throat felt dry, but there at school nothing was free.

For the second time that day, I felt my eyes stinging with tears. "I hate school," I said.

Mago watched a boy in my class heading toward us eating a mango-on-a-stick. She gasped when the boy dropped his mango onto the ground. He reached for it, but then stood up and left it there, walking away in disappointment. I looked at Mago and knew what she was thinking.

Every time we went out to run errands, she would look around for fruit or a lollipop some unlucky kid had dropped. Sometimes she got lucky. Sometimes she didn't.

Mago looked at the mango, and I knew she wouldn't resist it. "Go get it," she told Carlos as she pointed at it.

"You go," Carlos said.

"Some of my classmates are over there. They'll see me. Ándale, you get it, Nena."

"No," I said. She glared at me, and I knew sooner or later she'd make me do it. "Mago, you shouldn't eat things from the ground. They're bad. They've been kissed by the devil."

Mago waved my words away. "Those are just tales

Abuela Evila likes to scare us with," she said. Abuela Evila had said that when food falls to the ground, the devil, who lives right below us, kisses it and taints it with evil. "Look, I don't know if the devil exists or not, and I don't care. I'm hungry. So go get it!"

She pushed me toward the mango, but I shook my head. Tales or no tales, I wasn't going to risk it. But my mouth watered at the thought of sinking my teeth into the mango's tangy flesh.

The bell rang, and the kids rushed back to their classrooms. Mago and Carlos waved good-bye and disappeared from sight. I stood there under the jacaranda tree, and my feet didn't want to move. I didn't want to go back to the classroom and struggle to hold my pencil with my useless right hand. I didn't want el maestro to make me feel ashamed, evil. I didn't want him to hit me again and have my classmates laugh. But if I didn't go back, I knew I wouldn't learn to read and write. How could I ever write a letter to my parents and ask them to please, please come back?

As I made my way to the classroom, I noticed the mango again. It lay on its side, its flesh yellow like the feathers of a canary. It was covered with red chili powder and dirt. *And what if Mago is right? What if the devil doesn't exist? That would mean the left side isn't the side of the devil. That would mean I'm not evil for being left-handed.*

I looked around, and the courtyard was now empty.

46

I bent down and picked up the mango, flicked the dirt off it, and sank my teeth into it. The chili powder burned my tongue, and I felt warm all over. I stood there waiting for something to happen. I waited to see if the devil was going to burst out of the earth on his horse and drag me to hell with him. The jacaranda tree waved in the breeze, looking beautiful with its bright purple flowers. From above the brick fence I could see the colorful papel picado hanging in rows over the cobblestone street. The church bells started ringing, and I turned to look at the two towers at the top of the hill, the metal cross glistening under the bright noon sun.

I returned to class, and el maestro looked disapprovingly at me. I sat at my desk and looked at my pencil. From the corner of my eye I saw el maestro making his way toward me, his ruler going up and down, up and down. I reached for my pencil and clutched it tightly in my left hand.

7

Mago and Élida were in the habit of standing by the gate every afternoon to wait for el cartero, the mail carrier who came by on his bicycle. If he had mail for you, he would ring his little bell, a soft tinkling sound that could be the most beautiful sound in the world if only the mail were for you.

Instead the sound of the bell was like a little needle that pricked my heart because he never rang the bell for us. Always the tinkling was for Élida or the neighbors.

One day we watched him riding clumsily down the dirt road because he wasn't as good a rider as the baker. A box was tied to the rack on the back of his bike, and as he neared the house, the tinkling of the bell began. My heart was already breaking because I knew the sound wasn't for me. Élida pushed us out of the way and smiled at el cartero, her arms already stretched out to receive the box. Christmas was in two days. Even though in Mexico children don't get presents at Christmas but rather on January 6, the Day of the Three Wise Men, Élida said her mother had sent her a Christmas present because that's what they do in El Otro Lado, and her mother knew all about American culture.

But the box wasn't for Élida! El cartero handed it to Mago and then was off to the next house, like a fairy tinkling away as he disappeared into the distance.

"He made a mistake, that stupid man," Élida said as she tried to yank the box from Mago.

"There's no mistake," Mago said. Carlos and I held on to the box too, in case Élida tried to snatch it away. When she saw Mago's name on it, Élida stomped away and went into the house, calling out for Abuela Evila.

We opened the box to see what was inside. Presents from our parents! Papi and Mami had sent Mago and me two identical dresses. The top was white and the bottom was the color of purple jacaranda flowers. The collar was trimmed with lace and adorned with a beautiful silk orchid. We also got shiny patent leather shoes. Carlos got a pair of jeans and a shirt.

We rushed to my grandfather's room to put on our pretty clothes. But our parents hadn't realized that while they'd been gone, we had grown, as if somehow in El Otro Lado time stood still and over there I hadn't yet turned six, Mago ten, and Carlos almost nine. The shoes were a size too small, and so were the dresses. The sleeves of Carlos's shirt were two inches above his wrists. The skirt of my dress didn't even graze my knees.

"What do we do now?" Carlos asked, unbuttoning his new shirt. "Maybe they should have sent us some toys."

Mago hit him on the head.

"Ouch. What did you do that for?" Carlos asked, massaging his head.

Mago sat down on the bed and sighed. "I don't know," she said. She looked down at the dirt floor, and I wondered what she was thinking. I glanced at the shoes, and part of me was desperate to wear them. They were new. They had been sent to us by our parents. They were from the U.S.! But then I thought about my parents. The fact that they didn't even know what size shoe I wore made me want to throw the shoes into the trash.

We looked at each other. At that moment we all realized that the distance between us and our parents was tearing us apart.

Mago stood up and said, "Come on, Nena. Let's wash our feet." So we washed off the dirt caked onto our feet, and we put on the beautiful shiny shoes. "Curl your toes inward," Mago said. I curled my toes, and that way the shoes didn't hurt as much.

Mago, Carlos, and I held hands and we started spinning around in a circle, turning and turning, blending into a blur of purple, pink, white, and blue. Then, without letting go, we ran out of the house, out into the street, laughing and crying at the same time.

And as we ran past Don Bartolo's store, then cut across the vacant lot, then headed to the church, past the tortilla mill, and then past our old house, everyone stared at our beautiful new clothes, and not once did anyone say "poor little orphans." Our neighbors admired our pretty clothes and shoes from afar, not knowing that by the time we got home, our feet would be covered with blisters.

8

Four years after Papi left for the United States, and two years after Mami left, the construction of our house finally began. Which could only mean one thing—my parents would soon be back!

Papi had told us about his dream house in the letters he had sent to Mami from El Otro Lado. The house would be made of brick, with a shiny concrete floor. It would have three rooms, tall wide windows to let in the sunlight, and walls painted the color of Mami's blue eye shadow.

He wanted a house with a television, a stereo, a refrigerator, and a stove. A house with electricity, gas, and running water, and maybe even an indoor bathroom, one with a shower that made you feel as if you were standing in the rain on a sticky, hot summer day.

My grandmother had given my father a piece of her property, so our house was going to be built next to hers. Mago, Carlos, and I weren't happy about that. We didn't want to live next to Abuela Evila! But it would save my parents money, so it was the only option they had.

Workers came early one morning to tear down the outhouse and the shack in which I'd been born. I stood there watching, feeling sad that my little shack was being destroyed. Mago put an arm around me and said, "Just think about what is going to be built right there on that spot."

The workers returned the next day and the day after and the day after and began to lay the foundation, and after that, the walls. As soon as school let out, Mago, Carlos, and I ran down the hill to help. Carlos worked especially hard. He was quick and steady with the bricks and the buckets of mortar.

We scraped our fingers carrying bricks. At night we couldn't sleep from being so sore, but every day we put all of our energy into building our house, and when our fingers hurt too much, or our knees wanted to buckle from under us as we carried buckets of wet mortar to the bricklayers, we would tell ourselves that the faster we worked, the faster we would have a family again. That thought gave us strength.

But it wasn't long before the workers stopped coming. By the time February came to an end and Carlos turned nine, the workers were nowhere in sight. Abuela Evila said, "Your parents have no more money, so the house has to wait." We stood by the door every morning before going to school, hoping to see the truck that brought the construction workers coming down the dirt road. Then we headed to school, where all we did was look out the window and sigh the hours away, leaning our sorrow on our elbows.

By the end of the week, Mago stopped looking down the dirt road. She pushed Carlos and me up the hill and said that it didn't matter anyway. No matter how many bricks and buckets of mortar we helped carry, the house would never be done because it was just a foolish dream, just as silly as our dream of having a real family again.

"It will get finished!" Carlos said. "They will come back!" He took off running up the hill, and by the time we got to the gate of our school, he was nowhere in sight.

When we got back from school, I went inside to look at the Man Behind the Glass. "How much longer? How much longer will you be gone?" As always, there was no answer.

9

Scorpions had always been a part of our lives. Mami had taught us to check our shoes before putting them on in the morning, or to shake our bed covers at night in case there were scorpions in the folds. We had to shake our clothes before putting them on. We couldn't lean against walls. We couldn't reach into the wardrobe or drawers without fear of being stung by a scorpion hiding in the dark.

But at night, while we were sleeping, there was nothing we could do to keep a scorpion from crawling up the bed or falling from the ceiling.

One night I woke up screaming, my butt hurting as if I'd been branded by a red-hot poker like the cows at the dairy farm down the road. I recognized the pain right away. "Mami! Mami!" I yelled.

"Nena, what's wrong?" Mago asked.

"Scorpion," I said.

Mago ran out of the room to get help. Carlos jumped out of bed and stayed by my side but didn't touch me, as if afraid the scorpion would sting him, too. My grandfather kept on snoring in his bed and didn't wake up to help.

"Mami!" I cried out again. My mother didn't come to my side. In my pain, I had forgotten she wasn't here. It was my aunt who came running into the room, asking me where it hurt.

The scorpion was hidden on the collar of my dress, and when Tía Emperatriz pulled it off, I felt another sting on my neck. The pain spread up, pulsing in waves from my neck to my shoulders and up to my face.

"Mago, go slice an onion and get the rubbing alcohol!" Tía Emperatriz said. Mago ran to the kitchen while my aunt and Carlos hunted for the scorpion. The locals believed that if you killed the scorpion that stung you, its venom wouldn't be as powerful.

"What's all the fuss about?" Abuela Evila said as she stood by the door, rubbing her eyes. When Tía Emperatriz told her about the scorpion, Abuela Evila glanced around the room. "There it is," she said, pointing to the straw-colored scorpion crawling high up on the wall, barely visible in the weak light from the bare bulb hanging above us. Everyone gasped as it squeezed its flat body through a hole in the adobe bricks and disappeared from sight.

Tía Emperatriz rubbed alcohol over the stung areas and tied onion slices onto them with strips of cloth. Tears bathed my face. I felt as if a thousand hot needles were digging into my body. My face, my hands, and my feet were becoming numb. Tía Emperatriz forced me to swal-

56

low a raw egg. "The egg will keep the poison from hurting you," she said.

"We need to take her to the doctor," Mago said as she sat next to me and squeezed my hand.

"There's no money for that," Abuela Evila responded.

"The venom might not do much harm, now that she's eaten the egg," my aunt said. "Besides, look at you, Mago. When you've been stung, it's as if nothing happened."

"But that's because my blood is hot and strong," Mago said proudly. "And I'm a Scorpio, so scorpions don't do anything to me. But please, Tía, take Reyna to the doctor."

"There's no money," Abuela Evila said again.

"I'll keep an eye on her tonight," Tía Emperatriz said. "If she's still not well in the morning, I'll take her in. Now go back to bed, you two." Tía Emperatriz picked me up and took me to the living room, where she slept on a bed tucked into a corner. She lay down next to me, and I eventually fell asleep in her arms.

In the morning the whole room spun around me. I couldn't get up, and every time I tried to, I felt like throwing up. When I finally managed to get up, I was zigzagging two steps one way, one step the other way.

My aunt missed work to look after me. I felt as if I had a guitar inside my head. She held me tight by the waist and walked me to the outhouse, but with every step I took, the guitar in my head strummed and strummed,

57

the vibrations sending waves of pain that bounced inside the walls of my brain.

"She needs to see the doctor, Amá," my aunt said to Abuela Evila. "She's burning up with fever. Let's not take any chances. If anything happens to her, Natalio—"

"He and Juana chose to leave their children behind," Abuela Evila said as she cleaned the beans. "I didn't ask for this. Look at me. I'm seventy-one years old. Do I look like I need to be taking care of three young children on top of the one I'm already looking after?"

"They left so they could build them a house, Amá," Tía Emperatriz said.

"They won't come back. Trust me," Abuela Evila said, taking money out of her purse. "Look at María Félix. It's been nine years, and every time Élida asks her when she's finally coming back, she gives her excuses as to why she can't yet. But that's all they are. Excuses. And then it's me who has to dry the tears, who has to find ways to lessen the pain."

We waited at the end of the dirt road for a taxi. Despite my dizziness and shivers, I looked forward to the taxi ride. I rarely got to ride in a car, or go anywhere outside of the neighborhood. On the way to the doctor, I asked Tía Emperatriz if she thought Abuela Evila was right. "Do you think my parents won't come back?"

"I don't know, Reyna," she said. "From what I've heard, El Otro Lado is a very beautiful place. But here . . ." She waved her hand for me to look outside the cab window. I saw the banks of the canal lined with trash, the debris floating in the water, the crumbling adobe houses, the shacks made of sticks, barefoot children with bellies swollen with tapeworm, the piles of drying horse poop on the dirt road, the flea-bitten stray dogs lying under the shade of trees, flies hovering above them. I saw that, but I also saw the velvety mountains around us, the clear blue sky, the beautiful jacaranda trees covered in purple flowers, the bougainvillea crawling up fences, their dried magenta petals whirling around in the wind. I saw the cobblestone street leading up to the beautiful La Guadalupe church, papel picado of all colors waving over the street.

"Don't you think there's beauty here, too?" I asked my aunt. She looked out the window and didn't answer. As we made our way downtown, I continued to think that there was beauty everywhere around us. But when the cab stopped in front of the plaza, where I saw mothers and fathers strolling about, holding hands with their children, I realized it didn't matter what I thought of Iguala.

Without my parents there, it was a place of broken beauty.

Even though I felt better after the shot, Tía Emperatriz said I should sleep with her that night. I lay on her bed and watched her towel-dry her hair after her bath. She climbed into bed and turned off the light. It felt strange to have a woman's body next to mine. In the two years my mother had been gone, I'd forgotten how it felt to sleep with her.

I listened to my aunt's soft breathing. I wished I could close my eyes and snuggle next to her, bury my face in her hair that smelled of roses. But instead I moved to the other side of the bed, as far away as possible, and thought of my mother.

One day in class we were doing phonics, and the teacher wrote on the board *Mi mamá me mima. Mi mamá me ama.* We had to repeat after him as he pointed to the words. "Mi mamá me mima. Mi mamá me ama." "My mama spoils me. My mama loves me." My throat began to close up, and I wiped the tears from my eyes. When he said to write the sentences ten times, I couldn't stop my hand from shaking as I wrote the words down. And then I rearranged the words to make a question: *Me ama mi mamá?* "Does my mama love me?"

If so, why is she so far away?

I wished for the hundredth time that I had a photo of Mami. I was forgetting what she looked like, smelled like, felt like. I couldn't remember the sound of her voice, the way she laughed. Every time I closed my eyes to remember, I would hear Tía Emperatriz's laughter. If I took a breath, I would inhale the fragrance of my aunt's shampoo that smelled of roses.

10

The school year had come to an end, and to celebrate our good grades we were going to the movie theater for the first time ever! Tía Emperatriz was taking us to see the movie *La Niña de la Mochila Azul*, starring Pedrito Fernández.

We rushed to the community well to get water for our bath. When we got home, I only had a little water left in my buckets, my ankles were raw from being scraped by the rim of the buckets, and my palms were red and blistered.

But I thought about Pedrito Fernández, and I could hear him singing my favorite song of his: *"La de la mochila azul. La de ojitos dormilones."* "The girl with the blue backpack. The girl with the dreamy eyes . . ."

I was humming the song as we walked through the gate, and then I stopped when I saw the woman standing on the patio holding a little girl in her arms. The woman was wearing a lilac dress and golden high-heeled sandals that shone under the sun. I couldn't see her face very well because she had big sunglasses on. Her hair was curly and dyed a bright red. She looked like a TV star. The little girl in her arms was dressed in pink ruffles and lace. She was a chubby baby, her cheeks so puffy that it seemed as if her mouth were stuffed with cotton candy. I'd never seen such a healthy-looking baby before.

"Well, aren't you going to say hello to your mother?" the woman asked with a smile.

We stayed by the gate, holding on to our buckets.

"Don't just stand there," Abuela Evila said. "Go get your things ready."

Tía Emperatriz walked over to us, took my buckets, and whispered, "Go give your mother a hug."

We still didn't move from the gate. Mami was the one who came to us. I clutched Mago's dress and hid behind her. Mami didn't look like the mother I had tried so hard to not forget during the past two and a half years.

"Look at you kids. You've grown so much!" When she took off her sunglasses and I saw her eyes, I could no longer deny my mother. Carlos ran to hug her. I waited to see what Mago was going to do, so I could do the same. But she just stood there clutching the handles of her buckets. Élida left my grandmother's side and went into the house without another glance.

"Where's Papi?" Mago said. "Is he back too?"

"No, he's not back. Go and get your things so we can leave," Mami said.

"We're leaving right now?" I asked. *What about our movie?*

"Of course," Mami said. "Don't tell me you want to stay here?"

"I'll get our things," Mago said. She put a hand on my shoulder, and then went inside the house while Carlos and I stayed with Mami.

"I'm nine now," Carlos said, standing up as straight as he could. He was almost as tall as Mami. I kept staring at the little sister we had never met before. *She really does exist. She really is real.*

"Come here, Reyna," Mami said. I went to her, and I let her hug me with one arm. I hesitantly wrapped my arms around her waist, feeling as if this were a dream and she'd disappear at any minute.

The little girl pulled my hair. "Ouch!"

"Betty, no!" Mami said.

I moved out of the little girl's reach and massaged my scalp. Mago returned with our things stuffed into two pillow cases, and then we said our good-byes.

"Come back and visit," my aunt said as she walked us out to the gate.

Élida stayed in Abuela Evila's room and didn't come out to say good-bye.

"Wait! The photo," I said as we were leaving. I ran back into the house. Even though I'd memorized every part of his face, I couldn't leave the Man Behind the Glass.

The three of us sat in the back of the taxi, and Mami and her little girl took the front. We had so many questions to ask her, but didn't ask because the driver started a conversation with Mami.

"You're coming from El Otro Lado, aren't you?" he asked. People in Iguala always know when someone has been in the United States.

Mami laughed and told him yes. "I just got back last night."

"Did you like it? Is it as nice as people say?"

"Oh yes. It's beautiful," Mami said. "A truly beautiful place."

"So why did you come back? I mean, with our economy in the toilet, everyone is leaving for El Otro Lado, not the other way around."

Her little girl started to cry, and Mami didn't answer him.

We got off at the main road and walked the rest of the way to Abuelita Chinta's house in single file behind Mami. Dried bougainvillea flowers floated past us on the afternoon breeze. The air smelled of smoke, and I could see piles of burning trash on either side of the train tracks. We walked over the railroad tracks, the gravel crunching under our feet.

Abuelita Chinta's house was the only one on the block made of bamboo sticks. It was covered with cardboard soaked in tar on the outside, and the roof was made of corrugated metal. The neighbors' houses were made of brick and cement. The prettiest house belonged to Doña Caro. Her husband was a welder. He made good money, and

64

his family had a refrigerator and running water. Abuelita Chinta didn't have a refrigerator or running water, but she had a stove and electricity. She bought water from the next-door neighbor and carried it home in a bucket.

Doña Caro was sitting outside her house. When she saw my mother, she said, "Juana, you're back." I wanted to scream *yes, Mami was back and we would no longer be the little orphans!*

Our questions finally poured out.

"How is Papi?"

"Tell us about the U.S."

"What did you do while you were there?"

"Did you miss us?"

"Does Papi miss us?"

"Why didn't he come back with you?"

"Why don't you kids go outside to play with the new neighbors?" Mami said, not answering our questions. Only Carlos listened to her and went in search of kids to play with. Mami handed Mago the little girl and told Mago to take care of her while she and Abuelita Chinta prepared dinner.

Mago refused to take the baby.

"She's your sister," Mami said.

"She's your daughter," Mago said, and ran out of the house.

"Reyna, you take care of her."

"But—"

She put the little girl on my lap, and because I didn't

want to be defiant like Mago, I did as I was told. My grandmother's shack was just a big room with a bed, a table, a stove, and a hammock hanging from the rafters where my uncle Tío Crece slept. The bed we used to share with Mami was in the farthest corner. Unlike Abuela Evila's, this house had no interior walls, so privacy was hard to come by.

I sat on my grandmother's bed and watched her and Mami make rice, meat, and salsa verde. Finally we would start having real meals. Meals that were more than just beans and tortillas.

I was so happy about the food, I forgot I was supposed to be mad about watching Elizabeth, or Betty, as Mami had said we should call her. My little sister. A complete stranger. She was a year and three months old. She looked at me and smiled. Part of me wanted to smile at her. Part of me wanted to hold her tight in my arms and smell her scent of baby powder and milk, but I didn't do it. Instead I studied her face, and I was jealous that she was prettier than me and her hair was curlier than mine. Her eyelashes were thicker and longer, and her eyes were not slanted like mine but instead were round and framed by thick, dark lashes, so it seemed as if she were wearing eye makeup.

She was very dark, this little girl. A shade darker than Mago and much darker than me. It made me feel glad that she was so dark. I had heard people say that in El Otro Lado there were a lot of golden-haired people, with eyes as blue as a summer sky and skin as white as a pig's belly. But this little girl, who'd been born in that special, beautiful place, was as dark as the Nahuatls, the indigenous people who came down from the hills to sell clay pots at the train station.

Mami forgot I was there and didn't whisper anymore. Now I could hear a little of what she was saying to Abuelita Chinta. Something about another woman. A fight she had had with Papi. She was making green salsa, and as she talked, she smashed the roasted green tomatoes with the pestle so hard, the juice splattered onto her dress. But she didn't care. She said she hated Papi and never wanted to see him again.

"I'm going to get back at him, Amá. I swear."

"Hush, Juana. Don't say such things. He's still the father of your children," Abuelita Chinta said.

"But it can't be true!" I said. "Papi can't love another woman."

Mami looked up, startled. Realizing I was in the room with them—and that I'd been there all along—she got furious.

"What are you doing standing there? Go outside, and don't come back until I call you!"

Betty started to cry. I felt tears coming out of my own eyes, but Mami didn't care about our tears. "Get out!" she yelled, and I ran out.

Carlos was playing marbles with the boys, but Mago wasn't playing jump rope with the girls. I carried Betty in

67

my arms and struggled to hold her up. Her cheeks might have looked as if they were stuffed with cotton candy, but she weighed more than a sack of corn. Mago was by herself, staring into the distance, past the huizache trees, and when I looked in her direction, I saw the towers of La Guadalupe church near Abuela Evila's house sticking out like two fingers. Behind the towers the Mountain That Has a Headache rose up to the sky.

"Do you miss her?" I asked.

"Who, Mami? But she's back," she said. "And why were you crying?"

I started crying again. I didn't know why I still felt that familiar emptiness inside when I looked at the Mountain That Has a Headache, even though my mother was back. And why did it feel as if she weren't?

Carlos came over, smiling and pointing toward the house. "Can you believe she's here? Finally everything is going to go back to how it was before she left."

Mami poked her head out the door and told us to come inside. As I looked at her calling us over, I knew why the emptiness and the yearning were still there. Carlos was wrong.

The woman standing there wasn't the same woman who'd left.

11

The money Mami had brought from El Otro Lado ran out fast. Halfway through the summer she looked into ways to make money, but it was hard to find work.

"With this economy it's tough for everyone right now," Abuelita Chinta said.

By the train station was La Quinta Castrejón, a fancy place where wealthy people went to swim or have parties, even though it was on the outskirts of our neighborhood, which was as poor as could be. But La Quinta Castrejón sat there in our poverty, teasing us, reminding us of what we couldn't have. It was surrounded by a cinder block wall topped with broken pieces of glass. The driveway was lined with palm trees, the only palm trees in the neighborhood, like soldiers standing guard. Inside was a large swimming pool and three smaller pools for kids, and a playground with swings and slides and a seesaw. Weddings and Quinceañeras were held in the banquet hall every weekend.

"That place is immune to the recession," Mami said.

"People still have to get married. Inflation can't stop young girls from turning fifteen."

We started to sell snacks there on the weekends. On Saturday, after a lunch of alphabet soup and tortillas, Mami prepared the merchandise. At around five o'clock Mago, Carlos, and I left with Mami. Betty stayed home and cried. She wasn't allowed to come. Mami wanted her to come along. She wanted all of us to come so the guests at La Quinta Castrejón would see that she had four mouths to feed and would take pity on her and buy her merchandise. But the first night we went to sell, Betty got sick, and Abuelita Chinta said it was the midnight dew that had made her ill.

Mami said, "She's an American. This is why she's so fragile." But Mago, Carlos, and I had thick Mexican blood running through our veins, and neither the midnight dew nor the chill of the night would make us ill, so we had to come along.

We got to La Quinta Castrejón and were disappointed to see the other mothers setting up their stands. They had all their kids with them too. The winner was the mother with five kids, the youngest tied to her back with a shawl. Mami cussed under her breath and began to set up her stand. She put out the mint and caramel candy, little bags of peanuts and roasted pumpkin seeds, cigarettes and matches. Mago and I helped her with the stand while Carlos went around the parking lot offering to watch people's cars in exchange for tips.

70

We watched a limousine approach. I prayed it was a Quinceañera, first because I loved Quinceañeras and second because I didn't want to clean the outhouse if I lost the bet I'd made with Mago. The limo driver opened the door, and a young girl in her puffy pink dress and glittery tiara emerged. We watched her and her escorts walk into the hall while everyone clapped for her and congratulated her on becoming a little woman.

Soon all the guests were inside and we were out in the cold night shivering and blowing puffs of warm air into our hands. It was the middle of the rainy season, and the sky was thick with rain clouds. Once in a while lightning flashed over the mountains. Mami paid no heed to the weather. She rearranged her goodies, trying to find just the right way to display them. A man came outside to buy a pack of cigarettes, and he looked at Mami and at Mago and me. I put on my sad face, just like Mami had told me to do, so that he'd feel sorry for us and buy from us. But I knew no matter how hard I tried, I was seven, too old to compete with the baby nursing at his mother's breast. The man, who looked like a prince in his suit and tie, bought his cigarettes from the woman and even gave her an extra tip, for her children, he said, and then went back to the party.

I didn't look at Mami, because I knew she was angry, at me, at the man, at the mother with her five children, at Papi for putting her into this situation, at herself for leaving El Otro Lado in a moment of desperation. "I should have stayed," she said sometimes. "He left me there on my own, and I knew no one, but I should have stayed. There were jobs. Maybe not great jobs, but at least we weren't starving. And here in Mexico, with the cost of everything going up, how are we to survive?"

I leaned against the wall and tried not to think about that beautiful place she yearned for. Mami picked up her tray of cigarettes and gum and went into the reception hall to offer them to the guests. Sometimes she got kicked out. Sometimes, if the hosts were kind, they let her stay for a bit.

Mago and I walked over to admire the pool through the chain-link fence. From out here we could see the pool clearly, shining like a blue jewel. Above the ticket office was a white poster. The admission prices were listed on it, and Mago helped me add up the numbers because I hadn't learned to add big numbers yet. The cost of swimming here, for my siblings and me, plus Mami, was two days' worth of meals.

"Your father worked on those pools," Mami said from behind us, startling me. I turned to look at her, expecting her to be angry at us for leaving the stand unattended. I thought she'd yell at us, but instead she said, "Your father tiled those pools."

We turned to look at the big pool and admired the navy-blue tiles going all around the edge and covering the inside of the pool. "Papi did that?" I asked with awe. I knew Papi worked in construction, but I never really knew, until then, which projects he'd worked on around the city.

"One day he came home after work and told me that as soon as the pool opened, he would bring me here to swim." Mami put her forehead right up against the fence and looked at the pool. "As a thank-you gift the owner allowed the workers to come for a day to enjoy the pool, free of charge. So your father brought me here. Imagine that? I don't know how to swim, but your father does. He held on to me the whole time. I was so afraid, but not once did he let me go. . . ."

I turned to look at Mami and saw the pool reflected in her teary eyes. I wanted to tell her what Mago had told me once before. Memories are yours to keep forever. I wanted to tell her that as long as she held on to those special moments with her and Papi, they would always be hers, that other woman couldn't take them from her.

But Mami had already wiped her tears. She had already looked at the stand and noticed we hadn't sold anything. She walked away with brisk steps, her hands clenched into fists, yelling for us to come and tend the stand or there would be no money for food the next day. "I can't do everything by myself," she said angrily. "You kids are old enough to help."

I didn't move away from the fence. The music inside the hall drifted out into the cold night. It was finally time for the waltz. I looked at the pool Papi had tiled with his own hands and imagined myself dancing the waltz with him. In my mind's eye he was holding me tight, whispering into my ear how proud he was of me for becoming a little woman.

"Get away from there," Mami said as she pulled on my ear. She dragged me away from the pool and the pretty tiles, and I went back to tend the stand with Mago. Soon it was midnight and the rain was starting. The guests came out, rushing to their cars without another glance at our goodies. Carlos and the other boys ran from one car to another, trying to collect their tips from the guests. Some guests ignored the boys' outstretched hands and hit the gas pedal too hard. I worried for Carlos as I saw him jump out of the way to avoid being hit by a car.

"This is the last time we come here," Mami said as she threw all the goodies into a bag.

I had never liked coming here before, but now the thought of not coming back to look at the pools made me sad. "It'll be better next weekend, Mami," I said. "Maybe next week the guests will be different."

But Mami wasn't listening. She threw the bags onto our shoulders and folded the metal table and carried it over her head. Just as the rain began to pour, we rushed down the long driveway. We slid on the mud, our legs getting splattered by the cars. The guests turned right onto the paved street to go back to their fancy homes, and we turned left and stumbled on the dark, dirt road to my grandmother's shack. Mami wouldn't slow down even though we were gasping for breath and our legs were burning and our sides were hurting. She stared straight ahead and didn't look back.

12

In November, Mami found a job at a record shop downtown. She usually got home around seven, when it was dark. The road in front of my grandmother's house was made of dirt and covered with so many potholes and rocks that taxis and buses wouldn't come near the house. Mami had to walk from the main road to our house in the dark, since there were no streetlights.

One evening my grandmother sent Carlos to wait for Mami and walk her home. Usually my uncle waited for her, but that night he hadn't come home yet. Mago and I sat on Abuelita Chinta's bed and turned on the radio to listen to story time, where we got to listen to fairy tales and fables. Mami arrived by herself. "Where's Carlos?" we asked. Betty ran to Mami, wanting to be picked up.

"I don't know. He wasn't waiting for me," she said.

Mago and I looked at each other. I stood up and peeked out the door. There was nothing out there but the train tracks, the canal gurgling, the lonely whistle of the last train announcing its departure from the station. The wind rustled the branches of the trees. The fireflies played peekaboo among the bushes, and I wanted to go out and chase them, trap them in my cupped hands, and set them free inside Abuelita Chinta's house, where they could glow above us like stars.

"Let's go look for him," Mago said.

We made our way to the canal and peered into the darkness, but no one was coming across the bridge. We waited, shivering in the cool night breeze, chanting an "Our Father" under our breaths to keep La Llorona away, the weeping woman who roams the canal and steals children away.

"What if La Llorona got him?" I asked Mago, my eyes getting teary at the thought of my brother lying in the depths of the canal, never to be seen again.

Then we saw him making his way toward us from the other side of the bridge.

"Where were you?" Mago asked.

Carlos walked with his head hanging low. "Nowhere."

"What do you mean, nowhere? We were worried about you."

Carlos kept walking away, and we rushed to catch up with him. "Leave me alone," he said. He went into the house and didn't answer Mami when she asked him where he'd been. He didn't want to eat dinner. He lay down on his cot and didn't speak to us for the rest of the evening.

*   *   *

"What's gotten into him?" Mago asked me the next day. Carlos still refused to tell us what was wrong.

"I don't know," I said. I took a drink of cool water from the clay pot in the kitchen and ran back outside, where my friends and I were playing jump rope.

I loved Abuelita's street. In the evening the rays of the setting sun painted the dirt road the color of baked clay. Women sat outside their homes on wicker chairs, embroidering cloth napkins or reading a magazine while listening to boleros on the radio. In clusters or alone, men returned home from work. Some came from the corn- fields, covered with sweat and dirt, with their machetes hanging at their sides from a string of rawhide. Others, like my uncle, came from the train station, looking like ghosts, covered from head to toe with the powder that seeped out of the cement bags they loaded and unloaded all day long.

Back with Abuela Evila, we'd never been allowed out- side, and we'd only had one another to play with. But there with Abuelita Chinta, all the neighborhood kids came out to play. The train tracks provided hours of fun. We had contests to see who could jump over the most ties or who could balance herself the longest on the rails. Sometimes we put pieces of scrap metal on the tracks, and after the train swished by, we ran to pick them up.

As I jumped rope with my friends, I looked over at the house and saw Mago in there looking miserable. Even though Betty had taken my place as the baby of the family, Mago still treated me like her baby, and most of the time she refused to help with Betty. Sometimes she didn't have a choice, and whenever Abuelita Chinta had errands to run, Mago was left in charge of all of us, especially Betty.

As soon as Mami came home from work that night, Mago dumped Betty onto her lap.

"She's your sister," Mami said.

"But not my daughter," Mago said.

Mami shook her head and walked away. She helped Abuelita Chinta prepare dinner while holding Betty in one arm.

"Only refried beans and a chunk of cheese," Mami said. "That's all we're eating tonight?"

"There are people who won't be eating dinner tonight, Juana. Let us be thankful," Abuelita Chinta said as she scooped the beans into our bowls.

"I can't believe your father doesn't send any money for you kids," Mami said to us. "He's probably spending it on that woman!"

"Juana, we'll be okay," Abuelita Chinta said. "You're here now with your children. I'm sure that's enough for them."

"You're right, Amá. Things are going to get better really soon."

I got up and went to Mami. I wanted to hold her. I wanted to tell her I'd rather eat beans for the rest of my life as long as she was with me. But the look she gave me scared me. It was almost as if she hated me.

"You look just like your father," she said to me. I glanced at the Man Behind the Glass, and for the first time I was not happy to take after him. I didn't want Mami to look at me like that, a look full of pain, anger, hatred. I wanted to grab the Man Behind the Glass and toss him onto the railroad tracks for the train to shatter him to pieces. So Mami wouldn't look at him and look at me and think we were one and the same.

Abuelita Chinta set the bowl of beans onto the table and ruffled my hair. "Why don't you kids go buy some sodas? When you come back, the beans won't be so hot."

We took the money and left.

"So what's the matter with you?" Mago asked Carlos as soon as we were out of earshot.

"You're going to get mad if I tell you."

"Just spit it out," Mago said.

"Mami has a boyfriend," Carlos said.

"What?" Mago and I said at the same time.

"I saw her. I saw her with a man." He said that the previous night many buses had come and gone, but Mami hadn't come. He'd been afraid of standing there in the dark alone, putting himself in danger of getting beaten or killed by some crazy person, so he'd climbed up the tree near the tortilla mill. Minutes later a taxi had pulled up, and Mami and a man had gotten out. The taxi left, and as soon as it did, the man pulled Mami into his arms and kissed her on the mouth.

"They kissed for a long time," Carlos said. "I didn't know what to do. I didn't want Mami to get mad at me, so when they were done kissing, I just watched the man get a taxi and go. Mami started walking home, and I wanted to catch up to her, but I stayed up in the tree. I didn't want her to know I'd seen her."

"But what about Papi?" I asked.

"Papi doesn't love her anymore," Mago said.

"But why doesn't Papi love her?" I asked.

"Because he loves that other woman," Carlos said.

We walked in silence the rest of the way, the words weighing down on us.

At dinner I could see how much Mago was struggling to keep from shouting that we knew our mother's secret. She had a scowl on her face, and whenever Mami said something to her, Mago just grunted in response.

"What's going on with you?" Mami asked again.

Then Mago couldn't hold back anymore and said, "Mami, who was that man?"

"What man?"

"The man you were kissing by the main road."

Since Mami was holding Betty on her lap, it was hard for me to see the expression on her face. She buried her face in Betty's hair, as if hiding from our accusing eyes.

"Well, since you already know, I might as well tell you," she said finally. "His name is Francisco. He sells car insurance, but at heart he's a wrestler. He does

80

Lucha Libre on the weekends, and he's very good—"

"Who cares? What is *he* to you?" Mago asked.

"Don't talk like that to me, Mago," Mami said, looking over Betty's head. "Anyway, I might as well tell you now. I'm going away with him."

"What?" we all yelled. Betty started to whimper at hearing our angry voices.

"Juana, what are you saying?" Abuelita Chinta said.

"Francisco has gotten a contract to fight in Acapulco, and he asked me to go with him. I've accepted."

"But you can't go!" Mago yelled. She got up so suddenly, her chair toppled over. "You can't!"

"I won't be gone for long," Mami said. "Now sit down and stop yelling at me."

"You said that the last time," Carlos said. "And you were gone two and a half years."

"Mami, don't leave us again," I said as I rushed to her side.

"And what about us?" Mago said. "What's going to happen to us?"

"You'll stay here. Your grandmother will watch over you."

"Juana, you can't do this," Abuelita Chinta said. "It isn't right."

"When Papi hears of this, that you're leaving us again—"

"Don't you dare bring up your father, Mago," Mami said. "He left me. He left all of us."

81

"Juana, you need to think things through," Abuelita Chinta said above Betty's cries.

Mami got up and sighed, "I have, Amá. And I've made my decision."

When Mami left, she didn't even have the courage to tell us. When Carlos, Mago, and I got home from school the next day, we found Betty in tears. Abuelita Chinta told us our mother had just left with the wrestler. "They've gone to catch a taxi."

Betty's sobs were uncontrollable. Mago picked her up and held her. Carlos and I took off running, hoping that Mami and the wrestler might still be waiting by the main road. Carlos ran faster than me, and by the time I got there, he was bending over, crying. There was no sign of Mami anywhere.

13

After Mami left, Mago once again became our little mother and took care of us all. Betty missed Mami the most. She cried and cried for our mother, until one day the crying finally stopped. She wrapped her arms around Mago and clung to her with her chubby hands. I loved my little sister, and I didn't mind that Mago paid more attention to her than she did to me. Before, I used to think that since Betty had been born in the United States, she was more special to Mami. Now I saw that we were all the same to her. We were all just as easy to abandon.

Mago didn't want to talk about Mami. Instead she talked to us about Papi. Now more than ever she clung to the memory of him and told us that one day soon he'd come back for us. "Papi will save us," she said. "He'll be our hero."

The months passed, and Mami did not return. Abuelita Chinta was doing her best to look after us, but she didn't earn much as a curandera, a healer. It was hard for her to feed four children and herself. Since she was a respected and beloved healer, people would bring her fruit from their trees, like guavas, oranges, and plums, and she would give them to us. If someone gave her a tablecloth as a gift, she used that cloth to make dresses for us, saying her table had no use for such things.

"She's too old for this," Mago said one day as we watched Abuelita Chinta make her way down the dirt road to do a cleansing. Mago shut her textbook and said, "What's the point? Why study so much when we all know I won't finish school. I should just quit now and get a job. Put some food on the table."

"Don't say that!" I said. "You have to finish school. One day you'll be a secretary. You'll have a good job and make us all proud."

Back then Mago loved school more than anyone else I knew. Even more than me. Sometimes at night, when everyone was sleeping, she would tell me about her dream of going to tecÚical school and being a secretary one day. Being a secretary had once been Mami's dream. Mago would put her fingers in the air and pretend to type on an invisible typewriter. I would close my eyes and picture her dressed in a pretty silk blouse and black skirt with a slit in the back, the kind secretaries in soap operas wore. I imagined her boss, a handsome lawyer, telling her she was the best secretary he'd ever had. Then they would fall in love and get married!

Mago was almost a little woman. She was twelve now,

and the boys were starting to notice her. But she was very self-conscious about her scars.

"I'm ugly," she would say while looking at herself in the mirror.

To me she was the most beautiful girl in town.

The next day Mago left early and didn't tell us where she was going. She came back in the afternoon with a smile. "I got a job at the train station selling quesadillas. I'm starting there tomorrow."

"What? But what about school?" Abuelita Chinta asked.

"I'm still going to go. I'll go to my job straight after school."

Abuelita Chinta looked down at the floor and shook her head. "I'm sorry, my granddaughter," she said.

"Don't feel sorry for me, Abuelita," Mago said. "I want to work and help you. Oh, and by the way, my boss said that if there are any quesadillas left over, I can bring them home for all of you!"

The next day, when we were done with our dinner of beans and tortillas, Abuelita Chinta told us to go to the train station and wait for Mago. "It's too dark for your sister to walk home by herself," she said.

Carlos and I put on our sandals and left. I wondered if there would be any leftover quesadillas for Mago to bring home. My mouth watered at the thought of sinking my teeth into them. Carlos and I had a competition to see who could stay on the rail the longest. Soon we heard the rumbling of the approaching evening train, and we turned to see it snaking its way through the hills, shaking the leaves of the trees along the tracks. The conductor blew the whistle, and we scrambled out of the way. We rushed down to the dirt road and ran along with the train. It beat us to the station.

When we got there, most of the passengers had gotten off the train, and the few who were continuing on to Cuernavaca or Mexico City were boarding. We sat on a bench and watched Mago go from passenger car to passenger car carrying a tray of chicken quesadillas. She offered them to the passengers waiting for the train to depart. The whistle blew and the conductor yelled "Váaaaamonooooos!" but Mago was still inside the train. Last-minute passengers hurried to get on. "Come out, come out," I said under my breath. The train started to move, and Mago was nowhere in sight.

I stood up and rushed over to the train. "What are you doing?" Carlos said as he ran after me. The wheels of the train rotated as it pulled out of the station.

It would be so easy for Mago to stay on the train. She could decide to leave this place and not come back. She could finally say that enough is enough, she's tired of being our little mother. My breath caught in my throat, and I found myself rushing to the moving train, walking alongside it, searching desperately for my sister.

"Mago! Mago!" I yelled, tears streaming down my

86

face. Then finally Mago appeared on the landing of the last passenger car with an empty tray and jumped off just before the train sped up.

"I thought you were leaving me," I told her reproachfully. She laughed and ruffled my hair.

"Never," she said. We stood there as the train rushed past us in a blur.

14

Soon the school year was over and the rainy season began. I loved summers. I loved it when the rains were gentle and I could smell the sweet scent of wet dirt. Everything was green around me, wildflowers grew along the train tracks, and the clouds gathered at the peaks of the mountains like soft, cushy pillows. But halfway through the summer we got some serious rain.

For days and days the rain poured over us, with no end in sight. Thunder shook the bamboo sticks. We didn't have enough pans and buckets to catch the rain dripping through the roof. Then one day it didn't matter.

We woke up in the middle of the night to discover that the shack had flooded. Soon our bed was underwater. The only one who didn't get wet was Tío Crece, who slept on a hammock hanging from the rafters. He slept there all night long, while Carlos, Mago, Betty, Abuelita Chinta, and I sat on the small dining table and waited for morning. Mago held Betty in her arms and kept her warm while the rest of us shivered and leaned against one another as we drifted in and out of sleep.

In the morning the rain finally stopped. We spent the day getting the water out of the house in buckets. Our sandals got stuck to the muddy floor, and sometimes we fell into the water. We hung our clothes on top of bushes and on the rocks to dry. The mattresses steamed under the heat of the summer sun. When we finally got all the water out of the house, we took our buckets to the train tracks and filled them up with gravel. We went back and forth from the train tracks to the house, throwing handfuls of gravel onto the muddy floor as if we were planting corn for next year's crops. Finally the dirt floor was firm enough and no longer muddy.

Throughout the week we heard about the flood damage. The river running along the train tracks had flooded, the water spilling onto the bridge and making it impossible for anyone to get across to el mercado, the bus station, or downtown. The neighborhood next to ours was completely underwater, and the people there had to stay on the roofs of their houses. People navigated through the streets in makeshift canoes, and the corpses of their chickens, pigs, dogs, and cats floated in the water.

Later that week someone knocked on our door to deliver more bad news. We opened the door and saw a boy bent over, trying to catch his breath. He was barefoot.

His legs looked as if they'd been dipped in chocolate, and so did his hands and arms. I wondered how many times he'd slipped while running over here.

"What's wrong?" Abuelita Chinta said.

"Catalina," the boy said. "The river."

Tío Gary, my other uncle, lived across from the train station in a shack similar to our own, and the river flowed behind it. Catalina was his five-year-old daughter.

"Ave María Purísima," Abuelita said, crossing herself.

When we got to Tío Gary's house, all his neighbors were there, whispering to one another, crossing themselves again and again. Abuelita Chinta didn't go into the house. She hurried to the river's edge. The waters had receded, but the current was still swift and strong, dragging with it branches, broken chairs, clothes, pieces of wood. Farther down the river several men were holding on to a rope they'd tied to a tree to keep the current from dragging them away as they searched for my cousin.

"The current is still too strong," Abuelita Chinta said.

We went back to Tío Gary's house and waited with the rest of the neighbors. Catalina's mother, Tía Lupe, shook in pain. Her tears rolled down her cheeks nonstop, as if the river itself had gotten inside her body and was spilling out.

Tía Lupe said, "There's still hope. Catalina might have survived. She might have gotten hold of something to float on. She might have been saved by someone down the river." No one contradicted her.

The neighbors whispered the details to every new-comer who arrived. They said my five-year-old cousin had wandered off that morning to play by the river. Catalina's legs had gotten so muddy that she'd gone to wash them, but the bank was slippery, and she'd fallen in and been whisked away by the current. The neighbor's kid went to get help, but when help came, Catalina was nowhere to be seen. Tío Gary, who worked at the train station unloading the freight cars, came home as soon as he heard what had happened.

"They've been out there all day," the neighbors said. "And so far have found nothing."

In the evening we made our way home. Only the four of us left. Abuelita stayed to lead prayers all night long.

At night Mago and I couldn't sleep. "Tell me a story," I said to Mago.

"Which one?" she asked.

"Whichever one you want," I said. I just didn't want to think about Catalina and the river. I didn't want to think about her mother's tears.

"Once upon a time there were three little pigs . . ."

As I listened to the story, I thought about Papi's dream house. Maybe it wasn't so silly to want to live in such a house. I thought about the little pigs. The ones who got eaten were the two who'd lived in shacks of sticks and straw. But the one who survived the big, bad wolf was the one who lived in a brick and concrete house, just like the one Papi wanted to build for us. Maybe that was why Papi wanted such a house, to protect us, to shelter us from the horrible things outside our door. I fell asleep with a prayer on my lips for Papi to finish the dream house soon. Then he could finally come back, take us there, and keep us safe.

The next day Tío Gary and his friends made their way down the river for the third time. We stood by the bank and watched them get smaller and smaller. Inside the house all the women were back to praying. The kids stayed outside and found ways to entertain ourselves. We made tortillas out of mud. We wrote our names on the wet dirt with a stick. But our eyes constantly returned to the river.

Then the men finally came, their heads hanging low, their backs bent to the ground. They dragged their feet over the muddy dirt path, and in Tío Gary's arms we saw her, Catalina. Her limp arms hung at her sides. Everything became a blur. I wiped my eyes again and again, but the tears never stopped. Nobody touched Catalina except her mother and Abuelita Chinta, who pulled dried leaves and twigs out of her wet hair. Tío Gary said Catalina had been tangled up in the branches of a fallen tree.

They hung Catalina by her feet so that the river would drain out of her. We knelt and prayed, and not once did I take my eyes off my cousin's bloated body. I shuddered at seeing her like that, hanging by her feet, cold and lifeless. I was gripped with a fear so great, it took my breath away.

What if something happened to me, or Mago, Carlos, or Betty? What if by the time Papi finished his dream house, there would be no one left for him to keep safe? Or what if he never finished it, what if he never returned, and we were left here to face the wolf all on our own?

15

Six months after Mami ran off with the wrestler, they were in a terrible car accident. He died from internal bleeding. Mami escaped with a bad cut on her head where she'd hit the windshield.

Once again she returned to us with a broken heart.

During the two weeks after Mami's return, I would wake up to the sound of crying. In the thin moonlight streaming through the gaps between the bamboo sticks, I'd see her sitting on her bed, trembling as she sobbed. We didn't know how to comfort her or what to say, so we stayed away. She stayed away from us too, and only once did she try to hold one of us. Yet when she reached for Betty, my little sister cried and held her arms out to Mago.

"Why are you crying? I'm your mother," Mami said. But Betty just cried harder, and Mami had no choice but to give her back to Mago. She didn't try to hold her again.

"You have to give her time," Abuelita Chinta said. "You've been gone for many months, Juana."

94

"I came back, didn't I?" Mami said. The truth was that she had come back, but would she have done so if the wrestler hadn't died? Would she have come back if my father hadn't left her for another woman? We didn't know the answers to our questions, and we were afraid to ask.

Finally one day Mami sent Carlos to the neighbor's house to buy water from them on credit. After she bathed, for the first time since she'd been back, she stood in front of the mirror to put on makeup. She pursed her lips together, and I imagined she was kissing Papi through the mirror. With the bright red color on her lips, hot pink cheeks, and dark blue eye shadow, Mami became a different woman, and I could almost see that other mother—the one she'd been before she'd left—peeking through.

She combed her hair and wrapped a bandana over her head to cover the area the doctors had shaved to stitch up her cuts. She opened the dresser and took out her nicest dress. Then she sprayed on perfume that smelled of jasmine.

"Well, wish me luck," she said as she left the house. The four of us knelt at my grandmother's altar and prayed for Mami to find a job.

She came back with a smile on her face. Don Oscar, her former boss, had given her back her old job at the record shop, although she'd have to work the afternoon shift. "But a job is a job," Mami said, smiling. Even Betty, at three years old, seemed to know it was a time to celebrate, because when Mami reached out for her, Betty jumped into Mami's outstretched arms.

Mami said, "Let's go to el zócalo." We washed our dirty feet and faces as quickly as we could and then went out to the main road to catch a taxi. Mami asked the driver to drop us off at her sister's house. She lived downtown, close to everything. Tía Güera came with us to the plaza, and while she and Mami sat on a bench and talked, we played hide-and-seek with the other kids there. I remembered that whenever we had come here with Abuelita Chinta, it had been really hard for me to see all those mothers and fathers sitting there on the park benches watching their kids play.

How different it felt that day! While I ran and laughed and chased the other kids around, I would steal glances at the bench where my mother sat with my aunt, and I'd wave at her because I wanted to make sure I wasn't imagining her. When she waved back, I felt as if I were flying because it was so good to know I wasn't dreaming.

A few weeks later Mami came home full of excitement. She said, "The government is giving away land!" and hurried to gather the things we'd need to become squatters.

So Mago carried Betty, Carlos carried a rope, I carried a blanket, and Mami led the way with a shovel and a flashlight in her hands. We hurried to keep pace with Mami as we headed to the river. We came to a big meadow.

96

On the other side of the river was a grove of mangoes and tamarind trees. There were people at the meadow already staking out their piece of the land Mami said the government was going to give away very soon. Mami chose one of the few spots still available. Carlos gathered branches to use as posts. Once they were in the ground, we tied the rope from one post to the other to create one big square. Mami walked into the middle of the square, put a blanket down, and then sat and smiled. "Here's where we're going to live," she said. "I'm going to show your father I can build my own dream house too."

Mago, Carlos, Betty, and I sat next to Mami. All around us were families who, just like Mami, were there because they also had a dream. They were building tents out of torn sheets, cardboard, branches, and pieces of corrugated metal. Some even had a fire going and were cooking a meal out in the open. I caught a whiff of beans boiling, and my stomach growled. We hadn't brought a single thing to eat.

"So what happens now?" Mago asked.

"We wait," Mami said. "They didn't say when exactly the government officials are going to be coming by to give us the deed to the land, but it shouldn't be long. For now we can't go anywhere, or we'll lose our spot."

I turned to look behind me. The river was only about fifty yards away. I thought of my cousin Catalina. I didn't want to live this close to the river where my cousin had drowned. I thought of La Llorona, and how she always

97

roamed rivers, canals, and creeks. I didn't want to live anywhere close to water.

"I'm hungry," Betty said.

"Me too," Carlos said.

"Me too," Mago and I said. Mami shook her head at us.

"Think of this as an adventure," she said. She grabbed a stick and got up. "Here's where my room will go. Where do you kids want your room to be?"

Mago ran to a spot and said, "Here, over here, so that I can get a nice view of the river."

Carlos said, "I want my room to face the mountains."

I chose the spot next to Carlos because I didn't want a view of the river. But I did love the mountains.

"And here's where the kitchen will be, and the living room," Mami said, tracing the lines in the dirt with her stick.

But we couldn't be adventurous for long with empty stomachs. We sat back in the middle of the open land under the hot sun, with nothing to eat or drink. Finally Mami couldn't take our complaints anymore, and she got up and said, "Let's go home so you can have your dinner, but only you girls. Carlos, you stay to guard our land."

Carlos groaned. "But I'm hungry too."

"Don't you dare go anywhere. I'll come back with food and water for you," Mami said.

As we headed down to the tracks, I turned to wave good-bye to Carlos. He didn't see me. He sat on the ground scratching the dirt with a stick. I wondered if he was drawing the furniture for his bedroom.

*   *   *

Mami appointed Carlos as the head squatter, which meant he was responsible for watching our land. On the days that followed, Mago and I went to school while Carlos stayed by himself down by the river. He built himself a tent using branches, an old blanket, and pieces of cardboard. As soon as we got back from school, Mago and I rushed over to Carlos with a pot of alphabet soup or beans and tortillas. By the time we got there, Carlos was about to pee himself. He rushed into the nearest bushes while we laughed.

"Why won't they hurry up and give us the land?" Carlos asked. "I don't want to be here much longer."

Mami checked on Carlos as often as possible. She brought him caramel candies and lollipops, comic books, and a bag of little green soldiers to help pass the time.

"Any time now, mijo. Just be patient," Mami said.

"I'll be patient, Mami."

Mago brought Carlos the homework his teacher sent him every day so he wouldn't fall behind in class. We stayed with him for as long as we could, but as soon as the sun went down, Mago, Betty, and I got up and left. We waved good-bye and left him behind to guard the spot where one day Mami hoped to build herself a dream house of her own.

Then Abuelita Chinta said, "Juana, this is ridiculous. It's been two weeks already. How much longer are you going to keep that boy out there in the middle of nowhere?"

99

"For as long as necessary," Mami said. "A thing like this requires sacrifices."

Soon Carlos got sick with a cough, and Abuelita Chinta said it was the midnight chill and the morning dew that was getting into his lungs.

"What will you do if he catches pneumonia?" Abuelita Chinta asked.

"He won't. Any minute now we'll get the deed and have our own land," Mami responded.

But the next day Carlos was worse. He coughed so much that even the squatters all around him complained they couldn't sleep at night because of his coughing. "Take the boy home," they told Mami. She bought him some cough syrup and a little jar of VapoRub, and every day before going to work, she checked on him.

Abuelita Chinta watched with worried eyes, until finally she said, "Let's go and solve this problem once and for all." We went with our grandmother to the river, and by then Carlos was burning up with fever. He was sleeping on the ground on top of his blanket, and his arms were wrapped around his legs. He had wet himself too, and flies buzzed all around.

"Come on, mijo, let's go home," Abuelita Chinta said as she picked him up. Even in his feverish state, Carlos refused to get up.

"No, no, no. I'll help Mami with her dream house."

He was so weak, it wasn't hard for us to pick him up.

We took my brother home, where my grandmother immediately set out to heal him.

When Mami came home, she ran over to the river to save her land, but by then new squatters had moved in. She came back home in tears.

"I'm sorry, Mami," Carlos said. Then he buried his head in the pillow.

16

Not long after the government finally gave away the land Mami so desperately wanted, she decided to go live with my aunt. Tía Güera lived downtown, a few blocks from Mami's work. Mami had already been staying at her apartment a day or two a week. Then it had become three days, then four, until finally one day she packed up her clothes and said she was moving in with my aunt.

She got out of work late at night, when buses were no longer running. "The cab fare is seven times the bus fare," she said. "That's money we can use for food. If I stay at my sister's, I can walk there from work."

We begged her to stay with us. We promised we would be good. But Mami shook her head and said it was for the best.

She now visited us on Sundays, and every time she left, Carlos, Mago, and I would keep ourselves from running after her. Betty chased her like a little duckling. We were left behind to comfort our baby sister, to hold her while her tears subsided, to make funny faces and stick out our tongues, do cartwheels and handstands, sneak into the neighbor's yard to steal juicy guavas and mangoes to sweeten the bitter memory of the mother who came and went.

Finally it was Christmas again. I loved this time of year. It was the only time when our bellies would be stuffed with peanuts, fruit, and candy, thanks to the goodie bags we got at las posadas. These special celebrations were held for nine nights straight in our local church. All the kids received goodie bags and got to break a piñata. Sometimes if we were lucky, we even got a free toy on the last night of las posadas. But what I looked forward to the most that Christmas was that Mami was coming to spend it with us.

Tío Crece found a dried tree branch and sanded it until it was smooth. He painted it white and filled a coffee can with concrete and stuck the branch into it. When the concrete hardened and the branch could stand on its own, he brought it into the house and said, "Here's our Christmas tree!"

Since we didn't have decorations, we used eggshells. We painted them in different colors and hung them from our tree, which in the end no longer looked like a branch but a work of art.

Mago and I spent all morning cleaning the house. I sprinkled water onto the dirt floor and swept it until it was smooth like clay. Mago got rid of all the spiderwebs on the ceiling with the broom. We dusted the furniture and wiped the chairs and table, and we even went outside to sweep the dirt road. We wanted this Christmas to be special. Mami and Tía Güera were coming over in the evening, and we hoped that if we made the house look beautiful, maybe Mami would change her mind and decide to come back to live with us. This was the only Christmas wish I had—for my mother to come back to me.

When we saw them walking across the bridge, we ran to meet them. There was a man walking with them, and I thought it was my aunt's husband. I had only seen Tía Güera's husband once or twice, but when they got closer to the house, I knew it wasn't him.

"This is Rey," Mami said to us.

I turned to look at Mago, and the smile she'd had on all day long completely disappeared. I held her hand, but she pulled it away.

They came into the house. I smelled the delicious aroma of the roasted chicken Mami had brought. I looked at Rey. He seemed too young for Mami. She said she'd met him at work. I wished his name wasn't the male version of my name. I didn't want to have anything in common with this man, and I especially didn't want to share my mother with him!

Abuelita Chinta said, "The children are hungry. They've been cleaning the house all day. Please, let us sit at the table."

104

I tried to take a bite out of my chicken, but I couldn't taste it. All I could think about was that Mami had a new man in her life and now for sure she wouldn't want to come back to live with us. I made myself swallow. I didn't want to ruin our Christmas dinner.

Mago didn't care about that. A few minutes into our dinner she started to cry.

"What's the matter with you?" Mami asked.

"What's the matter? What do you think is the matter with me?" Mago yelled. "Why did you have to bring *him*? This is our night with you. It's Christmas. We don't need you to bring your boyfriends home!"

"I can bring whoever I want," Mami said.

Mago rushed at her, and for a moment I thought she was going to hit our mother. Instead she started kicking the chairs, pulling out her own hair, and screaming at the top of her lungs. It sent shivers down my spine. My sister had turned into a monster.

Tía Güera and Mami rushed at Mago and held her down, but Mago kept screaming. "I want to die! I want to die!" They forced her onto Abuelita Chinta's bed, and Mami and Tía Güera pinned her down while Tío Crece grabbed a rope. Rey stood by the door and didn't say or do anything.

"I want to die. I want to die!" Mago kept saying.

"What are you doing?" Abuelita said.

Nobody listened to her. I held Betty and my cousin Lupita in my arms because Mago was scaring them.

Mami, my aunt, and my uncle tied Mago's ankles and wrists. Mago kicked her legs up into the air and kicked Mami in the face before Tío Crece finally restrained her.

I had not noticed that Rey had gone outside. But when I looked around, he wasn't there anymore. The screaming suddenly stopped, and when I turned to look at Mago, her eyes were rolling back, and then her head hung limply to the side.

"She's fainted!" Abuelita said, making the sign of the cross. She rushed to get the bottle of alcohol. "Look at what you've done, Juana! You should be ashamed of yourself." My grandmother wept as she tended to my sister.

Mami's hair was a mess. Her cheeks were stained with mascara, and her hot-pink lipstick was smeared across her chin. She rubbed her cheek where Mago had kicked her, and I could tell it was swelling. Mami said, "I'm leaving now. If she isn't going to welcome Rey into this house, then I will not stay."

"Juana, be reasonable," Abuelita Chinta said, drying her tears. "You shouldn't have brought that man here. Not tonight. The children wanted to spend this day with you. Just because their father broke your heart and now you're looking for someone to mend it, it doesn't mean they aren't your children anymore."

"I'm sorry, Amá." Mami didn't look at us. She walked out the door and left. We sat on the bed, and finally Mago opened her eyes. She looked around and saw that Mami was gone.

"Come, children," Abuelita Chinta said, "the chicken is getting cold."

Carlos and I untied Mago's wrists and ankles, but we stayed there on the bed. Mago got up and headed to the opened door. I thought she was going to go outside and run to catch up to Mami, ask her to please come back. Instead Mago grabbed the door and slammed it shut.

17

One sunny day in May, my cousin Félix showed up at Abuelita Chinta's house. He was the son of Papi's oldest sister. He said, "Your father is going to call you in an hour. He wants to talk to you."

He turned around and ran off, and it took us a moment to recover from the shock. By the time we could speak, Félix was already hurrying across the bridge and turning the corner to head to the main road.

"Papi is going to call?" Carlos asked, and then the question turned into something else when he shouted at the top of his lungs, "Papi is going to call!"

We laughed and danced around in a circle. "Papi is going to call. Papi is going to call."

Since Abuelita Chinta wasn't home to give us money for the bus, we had no choice but to walk all the way to Abuela Evila's house. It was a forty-five-minute walk, cutting through fields of corn and sugarcane, and mango groves. We jumped across the canal and finally made it to the street that would take us to my grandmother's house.

By then we were all tired, and sweaty and panting for breath.

"Come on," Mago said. She wiped her forehead and then picked up Betty. Carlos and I ran after her. Not wanting to be the last one to Abuela Evila's house, I ran as fast as I could, but my side hurt and my throat was dry and my head was burning from too much sun. Then I thought of Papi and picked up my pace again.

Abuela Evila's house finally came into view.

"What should we tell him?" Mago said as we stood outside our grandmother's gate. There was so much to tell him, but how much time would we have before Abuela Evila snatched the phone from us, as she'd done many times before?

"Let's just tell him we miss him," Carlos said. "I think he has something he wants to tell us, don't you think? Or why would he be calling us after all this time?"

We knocked on the gate and waited. Then Élida came out and smirked. She glanced at us and shook her head. "You could have at least changed out of those rags," she said. "Look at you—you look like beggars."

"So what?" Mago said. "It's not like he's going to see us like this."

Then my cousin Félix poked his head out the kitchen doorway and laughed. He whispered something to Élida, and then she laughed too. We walked past them and went into the living room. I wondered what could be so funny.

109

Since he had left when I was two, I had no memory of Papi. But after the thousands of times I'd looked at his photograph, I knew every inch of his face. This was why when Mago, Carlos, Betty, and I entered my grandmother's living room, nobody had to tell me who the man sitting on the couch was. He had put on weight. He was wearing glasses. His skin was the color of rain-soaked earth, not black-and-white like in the photo. And he was made of flesh and blood, the Man Behind the Glass.

"Go say hello to your father," Tía Emperatriz said. She came up behind us and pushed the four of us toward him. I didn't want to go. All I wanted was to run away, run back to Abuelita Chinta's shack, far away from that man.

That stranger. My father.

I didn't want to see the look on his face, a look of surprise, shame, and pity. I knew he was ashamed of what he saw, of the children we were. Had he imagined us differently? What a cruel joke my cousin Félix had played on us by not telling us the truth! If he had, we would have bathed and changed our clothes before coming here.

Now I had to stand there, before the father I hadn't seen in almost eight years, looking like a beggar. My dress was stained and torn. My feet were clad in cheap plastic sandals and covered in dust from the dirt roads. My face was sweaty and sunburned from walking almost an hour under the hot sun to get here. My hair was matted and dirty. When was the last time I'd taken a bath? I wondered if Papi could see the lice running around on my scalp. I got an overwhelming urge to scratch. I bit my lips and tried not to move.

"Look at you kids. You are so big!" Papi said, walking toward us, since we four were too shocked to move.

"Mi negra!" Papi said, hugging Mago. She was thirteen years old and was almost as tall as Papi. Mago hugged Papi with all her might, as if afraid he would disappear. Next Papi hugged Betty, who was four years old and, like me, had no memories of him.

"Cómo estás, Carnal?" Papi said as he gave Carlos a hug. My brother couldn't contain his excitement at seeing Papi. I knew because he was smiling the biggest smile I'd ever seen, and for the first time didn't seem to care that we could see his crooked teeth. Unlike me, Carlos didn't care that we were filthy from head to toe. He didn't care that his jeans were torn at the knees and his shirt was missing almost all the buttons and his big belly full of tapeworm showed through.

I wished I didn't care either, but I did. In all the times I'd imagined meeting my father for the first time, I wasn't wearing rags, my feet weren't covered in dust, and my hair wasn't matted and dirty.

I searched every detail of Papi's face, just like I'd often studied his photo, and it made me feel good to see that I really did look like him. Papi called me over. "Ven acá, Chata," he said, using that special nickname Mago had

111

said he'd given me when I was a baby. All of a sudden I felt warm all over at hearing—for the first time—my father call me by my special nickname.

He's my Papi. He really is my Papi, I told myself. And I finally forced my feet to go to him. But he hugged me a little too fast and let me go before I had time to wrap my arms around him the way I'd seen Mago do. He moved away from me and turned to the woman who came to stand by his side. I hadn't noticed her until then. My eyes had been focused on him, only him.

"This is Mila," Papi said.

I looked at the woman who'd broken up my family. I wanted to yell at her, to say something mean, but I couldn't think of anything to say. She was prettier than Mami, and looked younger than her too, even though Mami had said that Mila was five years older than her. Mila had light skin and was wearing white pants and a pretty red blouse. Mami never wore pants, only flowery dresses like my grandmother. Mila didn't say anything to us. She gave us a weak smile and then turned to look at Papi.

Before any of us got a chance to ask him what we were all dying to ask him—*Are you finally coming back? Are we finally going to be a family again?*—Papi said, "I'm starving. Let's eat."

He gave my aunt money, and she went to buy a pot of menudo at the nearest food stand. Out of his suitcases Papi took three dolls, one for me, one for Mago, and one for Betty. They were life-size baby dolls with blue eyes that closed when we lay them down, and opened when we stood them up. I buried my face in my doll's blond hair and smelled the scent of plastic, the amazing scent of a new toy, which we hardly ever got to smell.

Papi gave us girls a couple of dresses and Carlos jeans and shirts. He looked at our feet. I put one foot behind the other, ashamed of my old sandals. My grandmother had no money to buy us shoes, so most of the time we went barefoot. These sandals were all I had, and right now I wanted nothing more than to burn them in the trash so that Papi wouldn't give me that look again, the same look the neighbors gave us when they called us the little orphans.

"I didn't know what shoe size you wore, so I didn't bring any for you," Papi said. "I'll buy you some tomorrow."

We played with our new dolls. Even though Mago said she was too old for dolls, she was more than happy to play with Betty and me, just to spite my cousin Élida. Papi didn't give her any gifts. She stood to the side looking longingly at our clothes and dolls, and part of me was glad that Papi hadn't given her anything. Now she knew what we felt when her mother visited from El Otro Lado and didn't give us a single present. But then I felt bad. I wanted Papi to be generous. I wanted him to be kind to his niece. Élida looked our way one more time, stuck out her tongue at us, and then disappeared from the living room.

Soon the evening came, and Papi still hadn't told us why he was here. *Is he finally here to stay with us?* I waited

113

for him to tell us he missed us. I waited for him to say he was sorry for being gone so long. I watched him sitting on the patio with his new wife, laughing at something she said. I felt jealousy running through me, burning sharp like a scorpion sting, and I thought of Mami. I thought now that I knew how she felt. Now I could almost understand her anger.

We spent the night at Abuela Evila's house. In the morning Papi shaved Carlos's hair to get rid of the lice. Papi also gave him a bath, as if my brother were a little kid. Papi said Carlos was in need of a good scrubbing. He took us girls to the hair salon and told the stylist to cut our hair short. I wanted to protest. I wanted to tell him no. But when I looked at him, I was afraid he'd disappear if I angered him. I was afraid he might leave again, and this time never come back. So I sat still and closed my eyes when I heard the hissing of the scissors. I cried silent tears. The only beautiful thing I had was my hair. Now with hair as short as a boy's again, for sure he was going to look at me and see how ugly I was. Now for sure he was not going to want me.

"Look at all the lice," the hairstylist said to her coworkers. Papi picked up a newspaper on the seat next to him and hid behind it. Mago sat with Betty on her lap, waiting. When the hairstylist was done with me, it was Betty's turn. She cried and moved her head, and Mago had to hold her still. When the hairstylist was done with Betty and asked Mago to sit down, Papi said, "Not her."

114

I looked at Mago, and I was so angry, I could spit at her. On our way home Papi stopped at the pharmacy and bought special lice shampoo and made us wash our hair with it as soon as we got to the house. "You didn't have to cut my hair," I told Papi, not able to hold my anger any longer.

He looked at me and said, "It'll grow back, Chata. Don't worry." I stopped being angry at Papi after hearing my special nickname.

Later Papi inspected the house he'd had built for us. After eight years Papi's dream house was almost finished. It just needed the windowpanes installed. As we walked from room to room, we told Papi how we'd helped to build his dream house.

"We carried the gravel in buckets," Carlos said.

"And the mortar," Mago said.

"And bricks. Lots of bricks," I said. I still remembered how much my fingers had hurt from being scraped and how my knees had buckled under the weight of the buckets of wet mortar. Now that the house was finished, so much had changed. My parents were no longer together. The family we'd once had was gone. *Can we ever get it back? Now that Papi is here, can I finally have that family I yearn for?*

"Which is going to be your room?" Mago asked Papi. He looked at us and sighed, but he didn't say anything.

In the evening, when Papi reached into his suitcase to grab his pajamas, he found a big surprise. A dozen baby scorpions, and their mother, came tumbling out onto the floor. I screamed and jumped onto the couch.

"You could've been stung," Mila said, scanning the floor as if to make sure he'd killed all the scorpions, and then she added, "Don't you think it's time we went home?"

Go home? But this is his home.

As if reading my thoughts, Mago said, "Our house is finished now. He doesn't need to leave again." She turned to Papi and said, "Right, Papi? You're staying now, aren't you?"

Papi looked at Mila, and then at us. "Let's talk about it later, está bien?"

"Why don't you tell them now, Natalio? Tell them you aren't staying," Mila said.

"All right," Papi said. He sat us down on the couch and said, "Well, you see, kids, I've decided I can't come back here. Even though the house is finished, there are no jobs here. If I come back, we'll still live in this miserable poverty."

"But the house is finished, Papi. At least we'll have a pretty house," I said. "That was the house you dreamed of, and now you have it. Aren't you happy, Papi?"

"We don't eat much," Carlos said. "You wouldn't need to make a lot of money to feed us. Mago already has a job at the train station. I could get one too. I'm old enough."

"No!" Papi said. "You need to go to school. All of you need to stay in school, you hear? Mago, what's this about you working already?"

116

Mago stayed quiet. Papi looked at her, waiting for her to say something. Finally she stood up and said, "Abuela Evila was right all along. Excuses, that's all you have to give us. Excuses as to why you can't come back!" She ran out of the living room crying.

I wanted to cry too. Papi was leaving us again.

18

The next day Mila and Papi told us they were leaving in a few days. Since she was a naturalized U.S. citizen, Mila was flying back. Papi, who had no papers and no permission to enter the United States, would have to hire a smuggler to take him across the border.

"I'm not coming back here, kids," Papi said. "I have a new life over there, and I don't want to give it up, but I know it isn't fair for you to not have a father. I thought your mother was taking care of you. Now I know she isn't."

I grabbed Mago's hand. She was my little mother. Even if Papi and Mami didn't want me, at least my sister did. Mago squeezed my hand tight. "Take us with you, Papi," she said. "If you aren't coming back, then take us with you."

"I don't have enough money to take all of you with me. I can only take one of you," Papi said.

I kept my eyes on the ground, afraid to look up. Tears gathered in my eyes because I didn't want to hear what

Papi was going to say next. I knew who he would choose. I squeezed Mago's hand more tightly, afraid Papi would yank her from me.

"I'll take Mago with me. She's the oldest, and she won't have as much trouble running across the border with me."

"You can't take her," I said. "You can't take her!"

"Why not?" Papi asked.

"Because she's all I have."

Mago looked at me and put her arms around me. I held on tight. I had survived being left by Papi. I'd lived through Mami's constant comings and goings. But if Mago left me too, I didn't think I could survive that. I looked at my father and wished he hadn't come back. I wished he'd stayed where he was. I wished he was just a photograph hanging on the wall. I would prefer that to losing my sister. Why did he have to come back, only to leave again and take away the only person who truly loved me?

"And what about me, Papi?" Carlos said. "I can run really fast. Just ask my friends. They can never catch me when we play soccer. I'll leave la migra in the dust!"

Papi put his hand on Carlos's shoulder. "You're right, Carnal. You could probably manage the crossing as well as Mago. I'll take you with me. But you, Chata, I cannot."

"How could you split us up?" I asked. "How could you take them away? How could you leave me behind?"

"I don't want to separate you," Papi said, bending down to look at me. "I will come back for you, Chata. I promise

119

that as soon as I have some money, I will come back for you."

I shook my head, unable to believe him. "The last time you left, you were gone eight years, Papi."

Papi looked down and didn't say anything.

We returned to Abuelita Chinta's house that evening because Papi didn't want us to miss school.

"You'll still be here tomorrow, won't you?" Mago asked. We were afraid that while we were gone, Papi would pack up and leave, never to come back to Iguala again.

"Of course I will, negra," Papi said.

At school my classmates wanted to know all about Papi. They asked painful questions I didn't want to answer. "Is he finally moving back here?" they asked. "Or is he taking you with him?"

I didn't want to tell them the truth. I didn't want to admit that Papi didn't want me. He only wanted my sister and my brother. So I started to lie. "Yes, Papi is taking me with him. Good-bye, my friends. I will miss you." I could see the look of envy in their eyes.

"You're so lucky, Reyna," they said to me.

By the end of the school day, I was starting to believe the lies myself. But then I was suddenly afraid. When my classmates found out I wasn't going anywhere, they'd make fun of me so much that I knew I'd die of shame, because they'd never let me forget that my father hadn't wanted me.

120

*   *   *

When we got to Abuela Evila's house after school, Papi and Mila were sitting on the patio with my grandmother. He called us over, and I was the first to rush to his side.

"Papi, you have to take me back to El Otro Lado with you," I said to him.

"Why is that?"

"Because I told my friends you would, and I've said good-bye to all of them!" I blurted. "I'll die of shame if they know I lied, Papi. Please take me with you."

Papi laughed. Mila didn't laugh. She glared at me.

"She's a stubborn one, isn't she?" Mila said.

"You leave her here with me, Natalio, and I'll teach her some manners," Abuela Evila said. "This girl needs to learn that bad things come to women who don't know their place."

"I won't go with you if you don't take Reyna," Mago said. "I mean it."

"Me too," Carlos said halfheartedly.

Papi gave me his hand, and I took it. "You really want to go live with me?"

"Sí, Papi. Please take me with you."

"All right. Then in that case, I'll take all my children back with me."

"But where in the world are you going to get the money?" Mila said.

"We'll borrow it," he said. "Beg everyone we know."

At first I thought Papi was drunk and didn't know

121

what he was saying. He said he'd call his friends and beg them to lend him the money he needed to pay the coyote—the smuggler who would sneak us across the border. He said it was a good thing Betty was a U.S. citizen and wouldn't need to be smuggled into the country. She could fly with Mila on the airplane.

For a moment I felt the familiar jealousy I'd felt when I'd first heard of my American sister. Being born in the U.S. was a privilege I wished I had.

"Will they shoot at us?" I asked Papi as we listened to him talk about the crossing, and the people he called "la migra."

"No, Chata, no. No one will shoot at us," Papi said as he sat me on his lap. "Don't be afraid." But I saw the way he glanced at Mila before hiding his face behind his beer can.

The next day Mago and I went to Mami's work to give her the news. Papi didn't want to talk to her himself. He said Mago might have a better chance of convincing Mami to let us go. He knew Mami hadn't forgiven him for what he'd done to her. At the sight of him, who knew what Mami might say—or do.

We walked into the record shop and saw Mami dusting the counter while dancing to a cumbia called "Juana La Cubana." We stood and watched her. Here was a side of Mami she didn't allow us to see. Here she was, smiling, dancing, singing, things I hadn't seen her do since she'd returned from El Otro Lado. I'd thought that part

122

of Mami was gone. Now I knew it was there, except not when she was with us.

Mami turned and saw us standing at the entrance of the shop. "You startled me!" she said, clutching her chest. She rushed to the stereo and turned down the volume. "So he's finally back, huh?" she said when we gave her the news. "And now he wants to take my children away from me?"

Luckily, Tío Gary arrived just in time. He calmed Mami down. He said to Mami what we couldn't say but knew to be true. "You aren't taking care of them, Juana. Why deny them the chance to go to El Otro Lado? Besides, our mother is too old to be taking care of your kids. Let them go, Juana. It's for the best. Don't deny them the opportunity to have a better life."

I held my breath and waited to see what Mami would say. Mami was a proud woman. She didn't give in that easily. *But maybe today, maybe today she will be different.*

"Fine," Mami said at last to my uncle. "If they want to go with him, so be it." I breathed a sigh of relief. She was letting us go! She turned to look at us and said, "Tell your father that he can't take Betty."

"But why?" Mago said. "You aren't going to take care of her anyway. Why won't you let her come with us? She's our sister!"

"And she's my daughter," Mami said. "If you three want to go with him, then go. I won't stop you. But I'm not about to lose all of my children."

123

"But—" I said. Then I couldn't think of anything to say, as the reality of our situation hit me.

If we wanted to go with Papi, that meant we'd have to leave our little sister behind.

"Come on, Nena. Let's go," Mago said. We went out into the busy street, and I turned to look behind me. Mami stood at the door of the record shop and waved good-bye. Too soon I couldn't see her anymore through the crowd of people rushing down the sidewalk. In my head I still heard the song Mami was listening to. I still saw her dancing in the record shop, her lips curved into a smile. I pulled my hand from Mago's and stopped walking. What if I stayed? Could Mami be that woman, the one in the record shop, when she was with me? Could she finally start being the mother she'd been before she'd left? Maybe she could, maybe she would, but if I left, then I'd never know.

"Nena, you coming or what?" Mago said as she held out her hand to me. I turned to look at my sister, and at the sight of her I knew I could never survive being separated from her. She was my Mago. How could I think of staying and lose the one person who had always stood by me?

I ran to take my sister's hand. I thought of my mother dancing in the record shop, and I promised myself that was how I'd always think of her, and I'd try to forget that other mother, the one who left and left and left.

19

We left early the next day. Abuela Evila cried to see my father leave again. I'd never seen my grandmother cry before. When I saw her holding tightly to my father, I couldn't help feeling sorry for her. All that time I'd only thought of my pain at having lost my parents. Now I realized that she was a mother who'd also suffered at seeing her children leave.

I thought about Mami and wondered if when we'd left her at the record shop, she had cried to see us go.

"We'll tell your mom to come back for you," we told Élida as we headed to the gate. She shrugged and sat down at her typewriter and began tap-tap-tapping away.

We took a bus from Iguala to Mexico City, where Mila would be getting off to catch her plane back to El Otro Lado. From there Mago, Carlos, Papi, and I would continue our journey to Tijuana by bus. The trip would be a little over two days. At first it felt like an adventure. I couldn't peel my eyes from the window. That was my first time leaving Iguala, and I wanted to take in everything. The bus went around and around one of the mountains, and we turned to look at the city spread out in the valley below. We waved good-bye to the city as the bus took the last curve and left the mountain behind.

By the next morning I was already fidgety and complaining from sitting for hours on end. Except for Papi, we were all suffering from motion sickness. We weren't used to riding in cars. The three of us sat in one seat in the middle of the bus. Papi sat all the way in the back because he said buses made him feel claustrophobic. I watched the sun weave in and out of the mountains. I wondered how many mountains we would have to cross to get to El Otro Lado.

"Wake up, wake up!" Carlos said.

It was early the next morning, our last one on the bus. I rubbed my sleepy eyes and looked at my brother. He shook Mago and me while tears ran down his face.

"He's gone, he's gone!" Carlos sobbed.

"Calm down," Mago said. We looked behind us and noticed that Papi's seat was empty. Where could he be? Mago stood up and headed to the front of the bus. She held on to the handrails and looked at every single passenger. Had Papi changed seats? Was he sitting in the front? Mago got to the bus driver and said, "Excuse me, sir, but my father is not on the bus."

"What? Are you sure?"

When Mago nodded, the driver said, "Well, I don't know where he is," he said.

That was when panic set in and Mago and I started crying too!

"He changed his mind about taking us to El Otro Lado," Carlos said, wiping his tears with his shirt.

"Of course he didn't," Mago said. "Papi wouldn't do that to us!"

"He didn't want to bring me in the first place," I said. "What if he did change his mind about me—about all of us?"

"But how could he leave us here in the bus, in the middle of nowhere? We don't know Tijuana at all," Carlos said.

I looked out the window, at the road that went on forever, the broken white lines running through it like needle stitches. "We don't know how to go back to Iguala. We don't have any money on us. What are we going to do?" I said.

"Stop it, both of you!" Mago said. "There has to be an explanation. Papi wouldn't leave us."

But he has left us before, I wanted to say but didn't.

We did the only thing we could think of—we started to pray. Abuelita Chinta had taught us that praying always makes you feel better, whether or not God listens to your prayers. Under our breaths we said an "Our Father" and a "Hail Mary." We asked God to please change Papi's mind and to bring him back to us, wherever he was.

*   *   *

When the bus pulled over at the next town, we were huddled together on our seat wondering what to do. One by one passengers boarded the bus. Others got off.

"We need to get off now before the bus keeps taking us farther and farther away from Iguala," Mago said.

"But how are we going to get back when we don't have money?" Carlos said.

"We can get off and just wait for Papi. I know he'll come. I know he will," Mago said. I wasn't as sure as my sister. Papi hadn't wanted to bring me in the first place.

Mago and Carlos looked at me. We didn't know what to do, and already the people had finished boarding and the driver had pulled the doors closed.

Just then someone banged on the glass doors, and the driver opened them again. A last passenger got on. It was Papi!

"Why did you leave without me?" he demanded of the driver. The driver shook his head, saying he didn't know Papi had gotten off. "You told us we had ten minutes, and you left five minutes later," Papi said. "I was buying breakfast for my children."

The driver pulled back into the road, and Papi made his way to us. I was so happy to see him, I wanted to hug him, but I couldn't bring myself to do it. Instead I smiled my biggest smile and told him how glad I was he'd found us.

He handed us our tacos. "They're cold already," he said. We were too hungry to care and devoured them in

128

seconds. Papi said he'd gotten off at one of the stops to buy food for us because he'd known we'd be waking up soon and would be hungry. He'd come back to find that the bus had left. He'd taken a taxicab to catch up to us. It had cost him a lot of money, he said, but what else could he have done?

"I'm sorry, kids," he said as he took the seat next to Mago.

"It wasn't your fault, Papi," Mago said, leaning against him. Then we all looked straight ahead, and soon there was a sign at the side of the road that said WELCOME TO TIJUANA.

20

Papi checked us into a small hotel. There was only a full-size bed, a night table, a dresser, and a television in the room. Papi said we three could have the bed. "I'll sleep on the floor," he said. The floor was tiled, and I knew it would be uncomfortable to sleep on, but he said a bigger room cost more. "And with any luck, we will only be here for one night," he said.

He left us there to watch television, and he went out in search of food and a coyote—the smuggler who would take us across. We watched reruns of *El Chavo del Ocho* while we waited for Papi. We'd never stayed in a hotel before, and we'd never watched TV in bed! For the first time I found myself beginning to enjoy our journey north.

Papi came back with tacos and sodas. "We head out tomorrow," he said. "Eat your food and then go straight to bed. We'll leave early in the morning."

The smuggler picked us up before sunrise at the hotel and drove us across the city. I was sleepy, and I found myself struggling to stay awake. I wasn't used to waking up that early, and I was groggy and grumpy. To make matters worse, that morning I'd woken up with a toothache, and Papi didn't have anything to give me. My tooth had hurt once in a while, and my grandmother had given me mint leaves to chew on. This time there was nothing I could do except doze off, hoping that when I woke up, the pain would be gone.

"Nena, wake up. We're here," Mago said.

The sun was just coming out when we came to a stop. We got out of the car and looked around. The border turned out to be nothing but dirt and bushes, rocks and weeds under a light blue sky.

"This is where we start," the coyote said. He looked at me and said, "Try to keep up, okay? You don't want to be left behind, do you?"

I looked at Papi. My stomach clenched at the thought of being abandoned in the middle of nowhere.

The coyote must have seen the terrified look on my face, because he laughed and patted my head. "I'm just teasing."

Papi's face was serious when he looked at us and said, "Stay alert, and do as the coyote says."

The coyote led us through a hole in a chain-link fence into the vacant land on the other side. We followed in silence. I looked at the ants scurrying around, gathering food. A hawk soared above in the wind. Birds chirped in trees. Lizards crawled under rocks. If I hadn't been so afraid, I would have been enjoying our adventure. But then I remembered that even though this place was beautiful, it was forbidden land. We were not welcome here.

Once in a while the coyote shouted orders to us, and we obeyed: Walk. Hide. Run. Crawl. I wasn't used to walking and running so much and so fast. My tooth began to hurt even more, and around noon, as we walked through the hills under the heat of the sun, I began to get a fever. Mago put her arm around me so that I could lean on her as we walked, but soon we found ourselves lagging behind.

"Come on, Nena. You can do it," Mago said.

"Maybe we should turn around and go back," the coyote said to Papi. He stopped and waited for us to catch up. "It's hard making this journey with children."

"No!" Papi said. "We keep going. She'll be okay."

Papi ended up carrying me on his back. I held on as tight as I could, branches grasping at me, as if trying to tear me away from him. I didn't remember ever being given a piggyback ride by Papi, and I wished we were somewhere else, like at a park, having fun. Not at the border. Not when I was hungry and sick and terrified of being caught.

My throat felt dry, and I asked for water for the hundredth time that day.

"Not right now, Chata," Papi said again as he struggled up the path. His breaths came in gasps. I knew Papi was getting tired.

Suddenly a cloud of dust rose in the distance, and before we knew it, a white truck was heading our way. "Run!" the coyote yelled. We rushed into the bushes, and I clung to Papi with all my might as he ran. He dove behind a rock. I gripped him so hard, I choked him. He pulled free from my grip and muffled a cough into his arm.

Had la migra heard him?

The truck pulled over, and men dressed in green, the men papi had called la migra, got out of the truck.

"Come out," they said. "There's nowhere to hide."

They took us to the border patrol station. Mago, Carlos, and I waited in the hallway while the agents took Papi into their office. We didn't know what they would do to us, to him. We waited, and waited. Our eyes hurt from too much crying. Agents passed by without looking at us. More and more migrants arrived. Mostly men and a few women, but no children. Even though they were just as afraid as we were, they looked at us, and they smiled, encouraging us. With their eyes they said to me, *Have faith. Don't give up.*

I didn't know how long Papi had been with the agents. I didn't know what they were asking him or what he was saying. But as the minutes went by, I began to wonder if they would ever let him go. What if they arrested him? Arrested us? What if we never saw each other again? I clutched my brother and sister as fresh tears came out of my eyes.

A border patrol agent with the bluest eyes I'd ever seen stopped in front of us and said something to us in English. We shook our heads, feeling stupid because we couldn't understand him and we didn't know how to tell him that. He smiled and went to the vending machine. Then he came back with sodas for us. He patted our heads and walked away.

I didn't realize until then how hungry and thirsty I was. I had been too afraid to think about anything other than Papi. We opened our sodas, and the sweetness of it gave me hope. It was a gift from a border patrol agent, from a gringo with kind blue eyes. Maybe the agents weren't so bad after all. Maybe they would understand that all we wanted was to have a family, and they would soon let us go.

It was a few more hours before Papi finally walked down the hallway to meet us. We were escorted out of the building, and soon we found ourselves back at the checkpoint near the border. We had to walk through a revolving metal door, and before we knew it, we were back in Tijuana.

"Let's get something to eat," Papi said. He took us to the nearest restaurant. I had never been in a restaurant, and even though we still didn't know what we were going to do next, I sat down and enjoyed looking at the menu and getting to pick what meal I wanted to eat. The table had a flowery tablecloth covered with plastic to keep the stains out. There was a jukebox playing rancheras, and the waitress was dressed in a pretty blouse with ruffles and lace.

I ordered fried pig's feet served with black beans. We hardly ever got to eat them, and I loved sucking on the bones. Papi made fun of me because everyone else had finished their food when I was still halfway through my meal, sucking each and every tiny bone of my pig's feet.

"I'm going to call you Huesitos instead of Chata," Papi teased.

I smiled at that new nickname—Little Bones.

"What are we going to do now?" Mago asked Papi now that our bellies were full.

I stopped eating. I remembered what the coyote had said, that with children the journey was harder. What if Papi thought the coyote was right?

"We'll try again tomorrow," Papi said, looking at me. I breathed a sigh of relief.

But the second time we tried to cross, we had the same bad luck. Again my short legs couldn't keep up with the others, and the heat of the sun's rays beating down on my head gave me a headache. Once, when we had sat down to rest, I walked away to pee in the bushes and found a man lying not too far from me. I thought he was asleep, but when I got closer to him, I saw the flies buzzing over him and the big bump on his forehead.

I screamed for help. Papi arrived first, followed by the

coyote and then Carlos and Mago. Papi told Mago to shut me up before la migra heard me.

"Is he dead?" I asked Mago as she took me away. "Is he dead?"

"He's sleeping, Nena. He's just sleeping," she said.

We got caught a half hour later.

21

We lay down to sleep even though it was only two o'clock in the afternoon. But that night we were attempting our third border crossing, and Papi said we needed to rest as much as possible. Tonight we wouldn't be sleeping. We'd be running through the night.

"This is the last time, kids," Papi warned. He lay down on the floor beside our bed and said, "If we don't make it this time, I'm going to have to send you back to my mother's."

"No, Papi, please!" I said. The thought of going back to Abuela Evila's house filled me with dread. I knew it was my fault. If I hadn't gotten sick the first time, we probably would have made it. If I had walked faster, run faster, not complained about the heat or my hunger, or hadn't asked for water, maybe we would have made it. If my molar hadn't been hurting me so much and I hadn't whined about the pain, maybe then we could have made it.

"I'm sorry, kids. I'm going to lose my job if I miss any more days." He said he didn't have the money to keep paying for food and the motel. He'd barely been able to borrow enough money to pay the coyote to take us across the border, and that money was being quickly spent. A big chunk of it had gone to the cab driver he'd paid to catch up to our bus.

"Don't make us go back there again," Mago said in a voice so soft, I didn't think he'd heard her. But after a minute or two, Papi finally looked at us. I grabbed Mago's and Carlos's hands and squeezed them. I thought about going back to Abuela Evila's house. Back to being an unwanted parentless child, back to waiting, always waiting, to hear from Papi so far away in El Otro Lado.

He sighed and said, "Tonight will be our last time. If we don't make it, you're going back. Now go to sleep. You'll need all your strength tonight."

But I couldn't sleep. I kept thinking about these past five days and how quickly they'd passed. I kept thinking about Mami, little Betty, my sweet grandmother—and I couldn't help feeling torn about our situation. I was happy Papi hadn't left me behind, but I was also sad about leaving my little sister. I felt as if we'd abandoned her. Why did it have to be so hard? I had to leave my mother, my little sister, my abuelita—to have a father. But now even that was in jeopardy. If we didn't cross this third time, I would lose my father!

Please, God, please give me wings.

Papi woke us up at sunset, and we took a bus to the meeting point where the smuggler was waiting for us. We crossed the dirt path, slipped under the hole in the fence, and immersed ourselves in the darkness that had quickly fallen around us. "Remember," Papi said, "this is the last time." He followed the coyote. We followed our father in a single file: Mago, me, and then Carlos in the rear. We walked along a small path, the thin moon curved like a smile. *If the moon is smiling at us, it must be a good sign, right?* Far in the distance I could see two red lights, like evil eyes. I shivered.

"They're just antennas," the coyote said when Carlos asked about the lights.

Every muscle in my body was tense. Every noise, like the chirping of crickets, the wind rustling the branches of the bushes, the sound of our labored breathing, frightened me. I thought those sounds were coming from la migra. I thought that somewhere in the endless darkness, la migra was there, ready to catch us and send us back to Tijuana, and ultimately back to Abuela Evila's house.

"Reyna, hurry!" Papi hissed. I sprinted to catch up to the group. I hadn't even noticed that Carlos had passed me.

At first it sounded like a kitten purring. Then the sound got louder and the coyote said, "Run!" In the darkness I saw him take off without us. My father grabbed my hand and ran too. I couldn't keep up with his long strides, and I fell. He scooped me up and ran with me in his arms. Mago and Carlos followed close behind.

A light shone in the distance, and the purring got louder.

"What's happening, Papi?" Mago asked.

"Helicopter."

Carlos tripped on a rock, but Papi kept on running and didn't wait for him to get up. "Wait, Papi!" I said, but Papi was like a frightened animal. He scampered through the bushes trying to find a place to hide.

"Get down!" the coyote said from somewhere in the darkness. Papi immediately dropped to the ground, and we became lizards, rubbing our bellies against the cold, damp earth, trying to find a place to hide. Pebbles dug into my knees. I couldn't see Carlos in the darkness, and I cried and told Papi to wait, but he pushed me into a little cave made of overgrown bushes. Mago and I sat by Papi's side, and he held on to us tight while we listened to the roaring of the helicopter right above us.

The beams of the searchlight cut through the branches of the bushes. A beam of light fell onto my shoe. I yanked my foot back and wondered if the people in the helicopter had seen my foot. I tried to hold my breath, thinking that even the smallest sound could give us away. *Please, God, don't let them see us. Please, God, let us arrive safely in El Otro Lado. I want to live in that perfect place. I want to have a father. I want to have a family.*

Finally the helicopter left. We could hear the chirping of the crickets once more, a howling of a coyote in the distance, and then we tensed up when we heard the sound of branches breaking.

Papi poked his head out of the cave and sighed in

140

relief. "I'm sorry, Carnal." We came out, and Carlos and the smuggler were standing right outside our cave. Carlos smiled, proud of himself for not getting us caught.

"You should have seen him crawl under the bushes," the smuggler said. "He's a real iguana, this one."

We continued our journey in the dark, and luckily, no more helicopters came by. I clung to my father's hand, and to Mago's hand on my other side. I didn't want to lose them in the darkness. We walked and walked, stumbling over rocks, feeling the branches of the bushes grasping at us, as if trying to hold us back. Then the coyote said, "We're here. Welcome to the U.S." I looked around, and in the dim light of the moon I saw the same bushes, the same rocks, the same dirt, the same sky.

What did he mean "we're here"? I wondered.

"This is where Mexico ends and the U.S. begins," the coyote said. But no matter how hard I looked, I couldn't tell how he knew that. It all looked the same to me. "The line is invisible," he said, as if reading my thoughts.

We finally got to the top of a hill, and the smuggler pointed to the lights of a city twinkling in the distance.

"That's where we are heading," he said. "San Ysidro."

The sight of that city gave me the strength to keep walking. If I reached my hand out, I could almost touch those lights.

We got to a huge road the coyote said was called a freeway. I had never seen such a big road before. "Follow

141

me," he said. "Quickly!" We dove into the ditch and waited. Cars sped by on either side of the freeway. "When I say run, you run!" the coyote said to us. "We have to get across unseen."

We crouched at the edge of the ditch, watching the cars, until finally there were no more in sight and the coyote said, "Run!"

We took off without another thought. I ran and ran, and in the darkness I did not see the divider wall in the middle of the freeway until I was about to crash right into it. Suddenly I was scooped into the air by Papi. "Careful!" he yelled. He tossed me over the divider, and as soon as he jumped over, he took my hand and pulled me along to the other side. We dove into the ditch just in time before the lights of the cars illuminated us.

"There goes border patrol," the coyote said. "We will wait here until it is safe."

Just before dawn we left the ditch and walked to the house of the second smuggler, the man in charge of driving us to Los Angeles. We arrived early in the morning.

"We made it!" I said, and Mago and Carlos and I jumped around with joy. Finally no more crawling through bushes, no more walking for hours on end. No more worrying about losing my father.

Papi got in on the passenger side of the car, and my siblings and I climbed into the back. The smuggler, a man named El Güero, said, "Lie down and stay out of sight."

142

"Even though we crossed," Papi said, "the danger isn't over yet. We can easily get pulled over by la migra on our way to Los Angeles."

And here I was thinking the danger was over. With a sigh Mago and I lay down on the backseat like spoons, and Carlos had to lie on the floor. My stomach growled. We'd gone the whole night without food.

As we drove from San Ysidro to Los Angeles, I wished I could get up and see what El Otro Lado looked like. I wanted to see with my own eyes the beautiful place that would now be my home. I started to get dizzy, and the only thing we could look at was the roof of the car. Finally the smuggler said we could get up for just a minute, to stretch, and what amazed me the most were the palm trees. I'd never seen so many palm trees. They were on either side of the freeway, whizzing by. The freeway took my breath away, so enormous compared to the tiny dirt roads in my town. And the cars were so clean and shiny, so different from the old rusty cars back home. I wanted the smuggler to slow down. I'd never been in a car that went so fast. My minute was coming to an end, and I wanted to take everything in. The last thing I saw when El Güero said to lie back down was a pair of golden arches. I wondered what they were.

"Can't we stop to get some hamburgers for my kids?" Papi asked the smuggler.

I'd never eaten a hamburger before, but I'd heard this was what people in El Otro Lado liked to eat. My stomach rumbled in anticipation.

143

El Güero shook his head. "Too risky," he said, and continued driving.

He took out a bag from the glove compartment. I watched him put his hand into the bag and then put something into his mouth. He opened the window and spat. He did this several times, and my curiosity grew more and more. He knew we were hungry, so he said, "You kids want some?"

Mago said, "What is it?"

"Sunflower seeds." He rolled down the window and spat again.

Mago, Carlos, and I looked at each other. Sunflower seeds? Here we were, coming to the richest country in the world, and this man was eating bird food? In my town I'd never seen anyone eat bird food before. *I'd rather be eating one of those hamburgers,* I thought.

"They're almost like pumpkin seeds," Papi said, urging us to take some.

Mago grabbed the bag from El Güero and put a pile of seeds into Carlos's and my cupped hands. She took some for herself and gave the bag back to El Güero.

"Look, there's the exit to Disneyland," El Güero said, pointing out the window. Then he remembered we couldn't see anything because we were still lying down. "You can get up now," he said. "I think we're safe."

Mami had mentioned Disneyland and how sad she was that she'd never gotten to go when she was here. I hoped one day we'd get to visit. I hoped one day I'd get to do everything people could do here, like speak English. With a big sigh of relief we sat up and got ready to eat our sunflower seeds. I let Mago go first. She put the seeds into her mouth and chewed them. When she swallowed, she started to choke.

"You're supposed to remove the shell," El Güero said. "I forgot to tell you that."

I put a seed into my mouth and did what El Güero had said to do, to crack the shell with my teeth and only eat the nut inside. It may have been my hunger, but those sunflower seeds were delicious. I sucked the salt off the shells before cracking them and eating the nut. For the rest of the drive to Los Angeles we munched on sunflower seeds.

I couldn't believe my first breakfast in the United States was bird food! But now that we were here, safe and sound, I knew I'd always think of it as the best breakfast I'd ever had.

Not too long after, Papi pointed to the tallest buildings I'd ever seen and said, "That's downtown Los Angeles." I thought about the map Mago had once shown me. I remembered the little dot labeled *Los Angeles*. It suddenly hit me that Mami and I had switched places, but the distance between us was just as big as it had been three years before.

"How far are we from home?" I asked Papi. "From Iguala."

"Home?" Papi said. "This is your home now, Chata."

145

I could hear the anger in Papi's voice, and I wished I could tell him that even though this was my home now, my umbilical cord was buried in Iguala.

The smuggler said, "Guerrero is about two thousand miles or so from here."

Two thousand miles was the distance between us and Mami. Between me and the place where I'd been born. I turned to look behind me as the car sped to its final destination. Mami had said she didn't want me to forget where I had come from.

"I promise I'll never forget," I said under my breath. We exited the freeway and arrived at our new home.

Part Two

THE MAN BEHIND

THE GLASS

1

Our new home in the U.S. was in Highland Park, a Latino neighborhood in Los Angeles. Mila and Papi owned a four-plex apartment building on Granada Street. We lived in the one-bedroom unit because we couldn't afford the rent of the bigger units. "First thing I have to do is pay back all the money I borrowed for the smuggler," Papi said.

For now Mago, Carlos, and I had to sleep in the living room until Papi repaid his debt. Mago and I shared the sofa bed, and Carlos slept on the floor. We didn't mind. To others, Papi's apartment may have seemed small, but to us, after living in a one-room shack with Abuelita Chinta and my uncle, it was a palace. The apartment had wall-to-wall carpet and an indoor bathroom with a shower and a toilet that flushed. It had real glass windows that let in the sunlight, with screens that kept mosquitoes out. Best of all, it had thick solid walls that made me feel safe and protected in a way I'd never felt before.

Outside was just as beautiful. There were no dirt roads. Only wide paved streets that seemed to go on forever.

There was not a shack in sight, only beautiful stucco houses with real shingled roofs, not roofs of corrugated metal sheets. There were no vacant lots full of weeds and trash, only lush green lawns and front yards with flowers of all kinds. I felt as if we'd arrived in paradise.

Mila took us to a store called Kmart. It was the biggest store I'd ever been to. It had the highest ceiling I'd ever seen, and the whitest and shiniest tiled floor in which I could see my reflection as I walked down the aisles. There were rows and rows of everything you could ever want, and clothes so beautiful that I wished we could buy them all. Mila said she didn't have much money to spend. She bought a couple of dresses and skirts and blouses for Mago and me, and pants and shirts for Carlos, a bag of underwear, and an extra pair of shoes for each of us, since our shoes had gotten ruined during the border crossing. We had arrived in the U.S. with only the clothes on our backs.

Since we arrived in the U.S. at the end of May, three weeks before the end of the school year, Papi didn't enroll us in school. He said we'd wait until September. So we stayed home all summer by ourselves while Papi and Mila were at the retirement home where they both worked. He was a maintenance worker, and she was a nursing assistant. We didn't mind staying home. Finally we had unlimited access to television! We didn't understand a word of English, but we soon got addicted to cartoon shows such as *ThunderCats, He-Man,* and *Jem.*

150

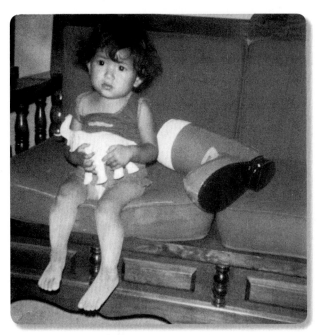

Reyna, at age two

*Mago, Carlos, Reyna,
and Mami*

Reyna, Carlos, and Mago

*Abuelita Chinta
and Betty*

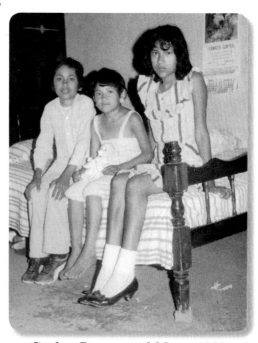

Carlos, Reyna, and Mago, 1985

*Mago, Reyna, and Carlos, recently
arrived in El Otro Lado, 1985*

Reyna, Carlos, and Mago's first time at the beach

Mila and Papi

Reyna in fifth grade

Papi in the United States

*Freight cars left to rust on the tracks
by Abuelita Chinta's house*

From top to bottom: Reyna, Mago, and Betty

Reyna at Pasadena City College, 1995

*Reyna and Diana at a
scholarship dinner, 1996*

*Reyna's graduation from
Pasadena City College, 1996*

Papi, Reyna, and Mami at the Quinceañera, 1992

Reyna at UCSC graduation, 1999

Mago, Carlos, and I also cleaned the house so Papi and Mila wouldn't think we were lazy. We swept the carpet with the broom because the one time Mago had tried to use the vacuum cleaner, it'd swallowed up the bottom of the curtains and we hadn't known what to do. The vacuum had starting smoking, and we'd pulled and pulled but it wouldn't let go of the curtain. Finally Carlos rushed to yank the cord from the outlet and we were able to get the curtain out of the vacuum. After that we decided it was safer to sweep. We knew how to use a broom. The vacuum cleaner was going to take some time.

But my favorite thing about summer was seeing the ocean for the first time! One day in late July my brother, sister, Mila, Papi, and I piled into Papi's red Mustang and headed to Santa Monica. When we arrived at the beach, Carlos, Mago, and I took off running. We stared at the immense sea before us. In my wildest dreams I had never imagined the sea to be like this. Miles and miles of water glittering under the summer sun. I breathed in the salty scent of the sea and stood there as the wind blew my hair around my face.

"Well, what do you think, kids?" Papi said as he came to stand behind us.

"It's beautiful," we said.

While Mila and Papi made sandwiches, Mago, Carlos, and I got a tan. Papi said we were dark enough as it was, especially his "Negra," Mago. But it felt so nice to lie under the sun, listening to the waves and the laughter of the families

151

around us. For the first time I felt like a normal family, a family with two parents, as I'd often dreamed. If anybody had looked at us, they would have said, "Look at that happy family." Things weren't perfect—I didn't have my mother or my little sister, Papi was still a stranger to me in many ways, and I still didn't know my way in this country and the American culture—but for now I was grateful for the small things. The beach, the sun, and my father by my side.

"Why don't you kids go play?" Mila said. Mago, Carlos, and I dug a hole in the sand and filled it up with water. The hole was only big enough to put our feet into. We looked for seashells along the shore, stood at the water's edge feeling the sand give way under us, but we didn't go in deeper. We didn't know how to swim. In Mexico we hadn't been afraid to splash around in the canal when it was waist deep. But here at the beach, with all these waves crashing down every few seconds, and the current pulling us in, it was hard not to be terrified of drowning in this beautiful yet endless water.

"You all better get in, or I'm going to take you home," Papi threatened.

Carlos and Mago went in deeper, but I stood by Papi's side remembering when I'd almost drowned in the canal and when my cousin Catalina had drowned.

"Come on, Chata. Go in," Papi said.

"I'm afraid, Papi." He grabbed my left hand and said, "Come on, I'll go in with you." Together we walked into the foamy water.

152

"Don't let go of me," I said to Papi as I clutched his hand, my toes digging into the sand eroding from under me. I tightened my grip on his hand, a hand that was the exact shape of my own with its long fingers. I still couldn't believe he was real. I still couldn't believe he was no longer just a photograph hanging on the wall.

"I won't let go, Chata," he said. I held on to my father's calloused hand and walked deeper into the water with him. I closed my eyes and thanked the saints for this day. This was the perfect way to see the ocean for the first time—holding on to my father's hand.

As promised, never once did he let me go.

2

As the months went by, Mago wrote letters to Mami and included the photographs we took with Papi's Polaroid camera. There were pictures of us wearing our new clothes from Kmart, of Carlos riding the used bicycle Papi bought for him, of us playing baseball in the yard. We took pictures of us posing on Papi's red Mustang (in pictures, you couldn't tell we still got carsick!), of us celebrating our first American holiday—the Fourth of July. In the pictures, we were smiling, as if life was more than we could ever have hoped for in this perfect place.

Through the pictures, we wanted Mami to see we were doing great and she shouldn't worry. We never told her about Papi's dark side. We didn't tell her that sometimes when he drank too much, he would yell at us and hit us with his belt. That was our secret. In the white area of the pictures, Mago always wrote: *To our beloved mother, whom we love and adore—despite everything. Your children, Mago, Carlos, and Reyna.*

*   *   *

Throughout the summer, I looked forward to starting school. I couldn't wait to meet my teacher, make friends, get my own books. Mila said teachers here in the U.S. didn't hit their students like in Mexico. Best of all, she said my teacher wouldn't yell at me for being left-handed. "That stuff your grandmother told you about the devil is pure nonsense," Mila said. When she said this, I started liking my stepmother, and I stopped being so afraid of going to school. I hoped one day I'd be like Mila, fluently bilingual and a U.S. citizen.

When September came and I turned ten, I started feeling afraid again. The next day I'd be starting fifth grade, Carlos seventh grade, and Mago eighth grade. I couldn't help feeling terrified! We didn't speak any English. How would we communicate with our teachers? How would we make any friends if we couldn't understand what anyone said?

But Papi wasn't worried about our lack of English. He was worried about something else.

"Don't tell anyone you're here without permission," he warned us.

"We won't, Papi," we said.

"I'm serious," he said. "If you tell anyone anything about how you got to this country, you can kiss it goodbye. You understand?"

Papi said we had broken the law by coming to the United States. I couldn't understand why there would be a law that prevented kids from being with their parents.

That was the only reason why I'd come to this country, after all.

"And you three better do well in your classes," Papi warned, "because if you don't, I won't wait for la migra to deport you. I'll send you back to Mexico myself!"

"We won't disappoint you, Papi," we promised.

"Está bien," Papi said as he finished his beer. "Well, off to bed. You have to get up early tomorrow. And I wasn't kidding about what kind of grades I expect from you."

We left the kitchen and went into the living room, where my stepmother was watching TV. At seeing us come in, Mila got up and headed to the bedroom.

Mago and I pulled out the sofa bed and lay down. Carlos usually slept on the floor, but that night, since he was anxious about the next day, he snuck into our bed. We huddled together while we listened to a helicopter flying very close to the apartment. For a moment I forgot we were at the fourplex in Highland Park. I was back at the border, running through the darkness, trying to hide from the helicopter flying above us. Once more I felt frightened, thinking that if we didn't make it this time, we'd lose our chance of having our father back in our lives.

"It's okay, Nena," Mago said, putting her arm around me. I snuggled against my sister, and the roaring of the helicopter faded away. "We're safe. Now go to sleep. It will be a long day tomorrow."

I tried to do as I was told, but it was a restless night for me. I still wasn't used to living in a noisy place. At Abuelita

156

Chinta's shack the nights were usually quiet, except for the occasional barking of dogs and the passing of the evening train. But here it seemed as if people never slept. Cars zoomed by on Avenue 50 at every hour of the day. Sirens echoed against the buildings. Helicopters roamed the night. Sometimes we even heard gunshots farther down the street from the gangs in the area. The only familiar sound I heard at night was the lonely whistle of the midnight train. That sound always made me yearn for my country and for those I'd left behind.

Early the next day, when Mago, Carlos, and I stopped at the corner to say good-bye to one another, my fear returned. Aldama Elementary was up the street. Mago and Carlos had to walk the opposite way to take a bus to Burbank Junior High School.

"Walk me there," I pleaded. "I don't want to go alone."

"It's only three blocks away, Nena," Mago said. "And Carlos and I are late. We'll miss our bus."

"Don't be scared," Carlos said.

"Everything will be fine. We'll see you when we get home," Mago said, waving good-bye.

I watched Mago and Carlos rush down Avenue 50. I wished I wasn't ten. I wished I was old enough to go to junior high with them.

I made my way to Aldama Elementary. I stood outside for a long time and watched children walk in. Some of them came in with their parents. All of them were strangers to me. Back in Iguala I'd known, by sight if not by name, almost every parent and kid who had gone to my little school.

Aldama was three times as big as my school in Iguala. I suddenly realized I had no idea where to go. I was so used to being with my sister, having her show me what to do, that now I was completely lost. I couldn't go through this by myself. I couldn't walk into this big school all alone!

A bell rang, and soon everyone was inside. I peeked through the main doors, and I was overwhelmed by all the doors, the hallway that seemed to never end. My school in Mexico didn't have hallways. It didn't have so many doors. Tears threatened to come out, and I was angry at myself for being such a useless coward. A mother walked by and asked, "Estás perdida?" At hearing the familiar Spanish words, I immediately confessed that I didn't know where to go.

She took me to the main office. The receptionist asked my name and called my classroom. A few minutes later a boy my age came in. The receptionist said something to him and motioned for me to follow him.

The boy didn't say anything to me as we made our way down a long hallway. We went into our room, and the teacher, a tall woman with short blond hair, looked me up and down and asked me something in English. I wanted to kick myself for coming late. Now I had to stand in front of the whole classroom while everyone watched as the

158

teacher spoke to me in a language I didn't understand! I looked at my feet. My toes wiggled within the new tennis shoes Papi had bought me from a place called Payless. I didn't like wearing tennis shoes. After ten years of walking around barefoot or with plastic sandals, my feet felt trapped within the thick material.

"Sólo Español?" she said. I looked into her eyes the color of the sea. I thought about our trip to Santa Monica beach, of Papi holding my hand. *Please don't let go of me, Papi.*

"Español?" she asked again.

"Sí," I said, relieved she spoke Spanish. The knot in my stomach began to loosen. "Me llamo Reyna Grande Rodríguez. Discúlpeme, maestra, por llegar tarde. Le prometo que no lo volveré hacer."

She shrugged and smiled. "No entender mucho," she said.

"Oh," I said, disappointed that she didn't speak much Spanish. She pointed to a table at the corner of the classroom and gently pushed me forward. I headed to the table. There were four other students there and a young man. He had black hair that was spiked with so much hair spray, it looked as if he were wearing a push broom on his head. He had a very skinny neck and a big Adam's apple that went up and down like a yo-yo when he swallowed.

"I'm Mr. López," he said in Spanish. "I'm Mrs. Anderson's assistant."

He had us introduce ourselves and asked me to go

159

first. "Me llamo Reyna Grande Rodríguez," I said.

He glanced at his roster and then looked at me. "Here in this country we only use one last name. See here," he said, showing me the roster. "You're enrolled as Reyna Grande."

"But I'm Rodríguez, too," I said. "It's my mami's last name."

He asked me to keep my voice down so I wouldn't interrupt Mrs. Anderson, who was speaking to a class of about twenty students. I wanted to tell him I had already lost my mother by coming to this country. It wasn't easy having to also erase her from my name. *Who am I now, then?*

"I'm sorry," Mr. López said. "That's the way things are done in this country. From now on you're Reyna Grande."

The students at my table laughed. One of them said in Spanish, "But she's so little. How can she be a queen, and a big one at that?"

Mr. López told them to not tease. He asked them to introduce themselves next. There was Gil, María, Cecilia, and Blanca. They were from Mexico, like me, except for Gil, who was from someplace called El Salvador. I didn't know where that was, but he spoke Spanish too.

For the rest of the day, I stayed at the table in the corner. Mr. López taught us the alphabet in English. It was difficult to pay attention to him. Mrs. Anderson was speaking loudly to her students, and it was hard for me to hear Mr. Lopez. Most of those kids looked just like me. They had brown skin, black hair, and brown eyes. They had last names like González and García, Hernández and Martínez, and yet they could speak a language I could not.

Whatever Mrs. Anderson was teaching the other students, it wasn't the alphabet. She wrote words on the board that I couldn't understand. I watched her mouth open and close as she talked. I wished I could understand what she was saying. I wished I didn't have to sit in a corner and feel like an outsider in my own classroom. I wished I wasn't being taught something kids learn in kindergarten.

"Reyna, pay attention," Mr. López said. "Now repeat after me. *A-B-C-D-E-F-G . . .*"

By the end of the day, I still hadn't fully memorized the alphabet and the numbers in English. I walked back home feeling scared. I thought about our trip to the beach, of Papi holding my hand. If I didn't do well in school, I wouldn't make Papi proud. It still hurt me that he hadn't wanted to bring me at first, and because of that I was desperate for him to one day say, *Chata, you have made me a proud father. I'm so glad I didn't leave you in Mexico and instead brought you here to be with me.*

But he wouldn't say that if I didn't learn!

Since I got out of school before Carlos and Mago, I had to go to the neighbor's house until Mago arrived to pick me up. Mrs. Giuliano lived across the street from us. She

161

was an old lady with hair like cotton and eyes the color of my birthstone, sapphire. Her sweet smile reminded me of Abuelita Chinta, although she wasn't missing any teeth like my grandmother. She didn't speak much Spanish, but she spoke Italian and English. She was the first Italian I'd ever met.

When she opened the door, she said, "Buongiorno, bambina!" She smiled and pulled me into her house. It smelled of bread and garlic. "Hai fame?" Mrs. Giuliano asked. She pointed to the stove, where she was making minestrone.

"Sí, tengo hambre," I said.

I sat on the stool, and she gave me a bowl of the soup. She asked me a question in both Italian and English, but I only understood the words "scuola" and "school."

"No good," I said, shaking my head. "No pude aprender inglés."

"No capisci?" she asked. "Dare il tempo, bambina."

Time? She was wrong. I'd never be able stop feeling as if I didn't belong in that classroom.

I wished I could tell Mrs. Giuliano that school wasn't the only place that was difficult to get used to. It was true we had lots of new wonderful things here in this country, but there were things we'd had in Mexico that we no longer had. Mago, Carlos, and I missed our freedom. We missed walking around the neighborhood and feeling safe. Everyone there knew us. The only person we knew here in Highland Park was Mrs. Giuliano, since she lived across the street. Also, because of the gangs in the area, Papi wouldn't allow us to go too far. Kids here didn't go outside to play in the afternoons. Women didn't come out to embroider and chat with their friends. Men didn't come out to have beer and play dominoes. The streets here were empty except for the cars speeding across Avenue 50. We had no one to play with except one another.

I didn't have the words to tell this to Mrs. Giuliano, but she seemed to understand how I felt and squeezed my hand.

After my meal Mrs. Giuliano took me to her backyard, where she kept chickens in a coop. As I helped her clean it, the smell of chicken poop and feathers reminded me of Abuelita Chinta's doves. The smell suddenly made me even more homesick for Iguala. I touched my belly button and remembered the bond that tied me to my mother and to my country.

Would it be so terrible to be sent back? Even though I liked this beautiful place, I still missed my home. It still called to me in different ways. Mexico was in the coos of the pigeons resting on the roof of our apartment. They reminded me of Abuelita Chinta's shack and waking up to the cooing of her doves. Mexico was in a cup of hot chocolate. It was in the smell of cilantro and epazote we bought at the market. Mexico was in the whistle of the midnight train traveling by Figueroa Street. Mexico was in the smell of wet dirt after it rained.

If I returned to Mexico, then I could see my little

sister, my mother, and my sweet grandmother again. I would also get to keep my two last names. I would be in a classroom where I understood what my teacher said.

But what about my dream of one day making Papi proud?

I stood there in Mrs. Giuliano's backyard feeling as if I were tearing in half. *Where do I belong?* I wondered. *Do I belong here? Do I belong there? Do I belong anywhere?*

3

When October began, Mrs. Anderson started giving us art projects to do, things like witches and black cats, ghosts and pumpkins made from poster and tissue paper. In Mexico we would have been preparing for the Day of the Dead celebrations. We would have been decorating our altars with marigolds and sugar skulls—and setting out plates of our dead relatives' favorite foods for them to enjoy. But here in the U.S. there was nothing like that to be done. We cut out skeletons, connected the bones with clips, and hung them on our door to announce the arrival of a holiday called Halloween.

The day before Halloween, Mila came home with a costume she'd picked up at the store for me. The plastic mask had a string on it, and the eyes were cut out so that I could see through the holes. The costume was of a girl with red hair and a purple star on her left cheek. The dress had sleeves the colors of the rainbow.

"Who is it?" I asked my stepmother.

"It's Rainbow Brite," she said.

"Who?" I asked.

Mila shrugged and handed me the costume.

"And what exactly is Halloween?" Mago asked.

"It's just a day when kids dress up and go from house to house getting candy," Mila said.

"You mean people give out candy for free?" Carlos asked, looking up from the mini cars he was racing on the floor.

Incredible.

I didn't worry anymore about putting on the costume. Whoever Rainbow Brite was, all I cared about was getting my free candy!

Mila had only bought *me* a costume because she said Halloween was for little kids. But at hearing about the free candy, Mago and Carlos wanted a costume too!

"We don't have money," Mila said. "You can share your sister's candy tomorrow."

Mago and Carlos went to bed disappointed. I hung my Rainbow Brite costume on the door so I wouldn't forget it for school the next day.

In the morning Papi's yelling woke me up. He was standing over Carlos, who was sitting on the floor where he slept. The living room smelled of Old Spice, Papi's favorite cologne, and something else, like the smell of vinegar and rust.

"I told you to stop doing that!" Papi said.

166

"I'm sorry, Papá. I won't do it again," Carlos said, trembling under his blankets. Now I knew what the smell was. Mago and I would wake Carlos up at night so he could use the bathroom. Papi would spank Carlos when he wet himself in his sleep. We didn't want our brother getting spanked, so Mago and I would try to help him. But the night before, neither of us had woken up and Carlos had wet himself, like he'd done since Mami had left us the first time.

Papi went to the bathroom and turned on the water in the bathtub. He came back for Carlos. "I told you not to wet yourself again. Maybe this will teach you."

"No, Papi!" Mago yelled.

Carlos didn't say anything. After five months of living with Papi, we had learned that Papi's favorite way of disciplining was hitting us with his belt. But Carlos didn't get hit that day. Instead Papi whisked him up and dragged him to the bathroom. Mago and I rushed behind them. The next thing we knew, Papi picked Carlos up like a rag doll and tossed him into the bathtub, pajamas and all. Water splashed onto the floor and the walls and onto Papi's blue work uniform.

"Wash yourself up!" Papi yelled. He picked up his car keys and headed to the door. Mila looked at us. She shook her head and followed Papi out the door.

Mago and I rushed to pull our brother out of the bathtub, where he was crying. Papi had only turned on the cold water, and Carlos shivered while we dried his hair

167

and helped him out of his wet pajamas. He didn't stop shivering even after he was in dry clothes.

"He didn't have to do that," Mago said.

"He left me for years. How can he treat me like this now?" Carlos said between sobs. Mago and I left the soiled covers soaking in the bathtub. We sat on the couch, not knowing what to do. I thought getting dumped into a bathtub full of cold water was worse than getting spanked, even though Papi's spankings hurt more than Abuela Evila's. It wasn't only because he was a man and could hit harder. It was because he was our father, our hero. Like Mago had once said he'd be.

"Come on, Carlos. We're going to miss our bus," Mago said as she got ready.

"I'm not going to school," he said, his bottom lip quivering. He was on the verge of tears again.

"Come on," Mago insisted. "You'll only make it worse. You know how Papi feels about school." They left to catch the bus. I stood there with my costume in my hands, the excitement of Halloween gone. I put Rainbow Brite back on the hook and left for school.

When Mila and Papi came home, he didn't say anything about that morning. I wanted him to say he was sorry, but we'd lived with him long enough to know that Papi never apologized for anything. He still hadn't said sorry for leaving us for eight years! He just walked past us and headed to his bedroom to change out of his work uniform,

168

which was dark blue pants and a light blue short-sleeve shirt with the word "Grande" embroidered over the left pocket. His hair had streaks of white in it, and I wondered what he'd painted at work that day. He never told us much about his job. But sometimes I heard him talk to Mila about their coworkers, or the old patients, and I wished I knew those people too, so I could feel included in the conversations.

"Why aren't you ready yet?" Mila asked me. I'd been sitting on the couch with Mago and Carlos for most of the afternoon. None of us had enjoyed the cartoons on TV, so we'd turned it off.

"Trick-or-treating will be starting soon," Mila said. "And it only happens once a year."

"We aren't going," I said.

Mila shook her head. "I know what your father did was wrong, but try to understand him. It's been a long time since he has had to be a father. Give him time to adjust."

Mila handed Carlos a white sheet she'd brought from work. "We already washed the sheets, Mila," Mago said. "They're drying on the clothesline outside."

"That isn't why I brought this," Mila said, grabbing a pair of scissors. She told Carlos to stand up and put the sheet over himself.

"What are you doing?" Carlos asked. Mila cut out holes over the area where Carlos's eyes would go.

"I'm making you a Halloween costume," she said.

169

A costume? Out of a sheet? She walked him over to the closet door so Carlos could see it for himself. He turned to look at us. Mago and I giggled. My brother was now a ghost. It was amazing!

"Let me find something for you, Mago," Mila said. We turned to look out the window and saw kids out there with their costumes on.

Mila came out of her room with the wedding dress she'd worn when she'd married her first husband. Mila had been married before she'd met Papi, and she had three children whom she saw once in a while. We didn't know the whole story, but we did know that Mila had left her husband and children to be with Papi.

Mila handed Mago the wedding dress. The satin had yellowed, and most of the sequins had fallen off. Mila's oldest son was seventeen years old, and the dress was older than that.

"I can't wear that," Mago said. "I'll ruin it."

"It's already ruined," Mila said. The way she said it made me think she wasn't just talking about the dress.

"Put it on, Mago," I said. "If we don't leave soon, all the candy will be gone."

Mago went into the bathroom and came out looking like a bride, and blushing like one too! After a good laugh, and taking pictures with Papi's Polaroid camera to send to Mexico, we got ready to go. Mila made us practice the words "trick-or-treat, trick-or-treat." The words were so hard to pronounce that we stumbled on the harsh sounds.

"Well, it will have to do," Mila said. She gave us a plastic bag each and told us to be careful. "Don't eat the candy until you get home. Your father and I need to make sure it's safe for you to eat."

The holiday reminded me of Las Posadas in Mexico. Except there we would only get a small goodie bag from only one house, and here the possibilities were endless! We walked from street to street, venturing into streets we'd never been to. "Treecotree! Treecotree!" we yelled as we knocked on the doors of the houses and the apartment buildings in the neighborhood. By the time we got home, it was past nine and our bags were bursting with candy. We had to carry them in our arms because the plastic handles had broken from all the weight, from the abundance only found in the United States.

Papi and Mila were sitting in the kitchen. We put our bags on the table, and they looked through our candy, throwing away the ones that seemed as if they'd been opened. Papi found a tamarind candy coated with chili powder in Carlos's bag.

"I used to like these when I was your age," Papi said.

"Here's another one, Papi. You can keep that one," Carlos said.

I waited for Papi to say he was sorry for what he had done that morning to Carlos. He didn't say sorry, but he did smile at Carlos and unwrapped the candy Carlos had given him.

"Thanks, Carnal." Papi patted Carlos on the back as they ate their tamarind candy.

171

4

"Reyna, your mother is here to pick you up," Mr. López said, handing me the slip from the main office. I gathered my things and ran down the hallway. *Is Mami really waiting for me? Has she come all the way from Mexico to find me? Does she miss me?*

When I entered the main office, a woman stood up.

"Ready?" Mila said, grabbing her purse. I followed my stepmother out the door, feeling stupid. I'd forgotten that Mila was going to pick me up to take me to the dentist.

For the past few months I'd had toothaches that had come and gone. Lately they had been getting more and more painful, until Papi had finally had to do something about it. The problem was, we didn't have dental insurance, and Papi said he and Mila didn't have money to pay the dentist. But Mila figured out a way around that—to use her daughter's insurance.

As we drove, I looked out the window and wished Papi was taking me to my appointment. He didn't want to risk losing his job by taking days off. Also, since he didn't speak much English, he felt uncomfortable going places. As a handyman, he was comfortable with a drill, a paintbrush, a wrench, and he could work in silence while his expert hands did the work. But outside of home and work, it was Mila who had to take care of everything.

As we neared the dentist's office, Mila reminded me what to say. "Answer to the name Cindy," she said. "And remember you're nine, not ten."

I nodded, remembering that Cindy was ten months younger than me. She was a lot prettier too, with long glossy black hair and beautiful eyes framed by thick eyelashes. She had only come to the house a few times, and when she came, she stayed by Mila's side and wouldn't talk to us or play with us. She wouldn't talk to Papi either and pretended not to hear him when he said hello to her.

I knew Cindy blamed Papi for breaking up her family. I knew she didn't like me, Mago, and Carlos because she thought we were trying to replace her and her brothers in Mila's heart. And I was ashamed to admit that she was right. Sometimes I did fantasize that Mila was my real mom. But those fantasies made me feel as if I were betraying my own mother, so I made myself stop. I knew Mila didn't love us—that she'd never love us the way she loved her children. Cindy had nothing to worry about.

I'd never been to a dentist. Abuelita Chinta would try to heal our toothaches with homemade remedies. I couldn't help feeling a little afraid now. In Mexico my grandmother had given me mint leaves to chew on when my molar had bothered me. I didn't think I was going to get mint leaves this time!

Mila and I sat at the reception area to wait. I looked at the pictures of a turkey, a pumpkin, and a pilgrim's hat taped on the door. There were similar decorations in my classroom. Mila fidgeted in her seat.

The dental assistant called out a name. When I didn't answer, Mila nudged me and stood up. I went into the dentist's room, and he asked me to sit down on a big leather chair. I jumped out as soon as it started reclining. The dentist laughed and said something in English while pointing to the chair. All I understood was the word "Cindy."

I sat there wondering how Mila felt about the dentist calling me by her daughter's name. The few times Cindy had come to the house, I'd noticed how uncomfortable she seemed around Mila. She didn't come very often, only when Mila practically forced her to. Mila's oldest son didn't visit often either. Her second son had never come over, not even once. They were angry at her for leaving their father for Papi. I didn't blame them. But now Mila looked at me, and she cringed every time the dentist called me Cindy. She scowled at me, as if she hated me for pretending to be her daughter.

Mila said my molar had a huge cavity and had to come out to let the new tooth grow in. For the rest of the hour, Mila had to translate for me what the dentist said.

"Open your mouth, Cindy."

"That's a good girl, Cindy."

"We're almost done, Cindy."

Mila didn't look at me when she translated. She looked at the wall.

While the dentist worked on my mouth, I fantasized about being the real Cindy, being Mila's daughter. Would she have willingly taken the day off from work to bring me here? Would she have not fidgeted, the way she was doing now while she waited for me? Would she have allowed me—just like she allowed the real Cindy when she visited—to go into her and Papi's bedroom without knocking, to lie down on their bed and watch TV? Would she have brushed my hair up into pigtails in the mornings? Let me sit in the kitchen and help her make dinner?

"We're almost done, Cindy," the dentist said, and maybe it was the grogginess from the anesthesia, but I really liked the sound of that name. I wished to never leave the dentist's office, because as soon as we walked out that door, I would once again be Reyna, the unwanted stepdaughter.

"Your daughter was very good," the receptionist said as Mila and I went out the door. Mila held me by the shoulders because I was feeling a bit dizzy and my mouth was numb and my lips felt three times their size. My lips throbbed as if they'd been stung by a scorpion!

"Thank you," Mila said. I waved good-bye to the receptionist and gave her a groggy smile.

On the way home Mila was very quiet. Was she thinking about her daughter?

"Are you in pain yet?" she asked as we pulled into the driveway.

"No, Mamá Mila," I said. Maybe it was the anesthesia that made me say that.

She took a deep breath and looked at me. "Just call me Mila. I'm not your mom, so you can't call me 'Mamá.' Just Mila, okay?"

With tears in my eyes I said, "I'm sorry, Mila. I won't do it again." Then I got out of the car and went into the house.

"That's what you get for being a traitor," Mago said when I told her what I'd done. "She's right. She's not our mom. Besides, she broke up our parents' marriage, and now you want to call her 'Mamá'?"

I lowered my head in shame.

Papi came home and asked about my tooth. I showed him the gap where my molar had been.

"I'm glad everything worked out," Papi said. Then he walked into the kitchen and sat at the table to keep Mila company while she cooked.

"I'm not doing that again, you understand?" I heard Mila say. Papi opened a can of Budweiser and didn't answer.

5

After not being able to watch television in Mexico, Mago, Carlos, and I couldn't seem to get enough of it now. Even though we couldn't understand English very well, we loved to watch *He-Man*, *ThunderCats*, *Transformers*, *Beverly Hills Teens*, and *Jem*. For the blink of an eye we also owned an Atari. One of Papi's tenants gave it to us after she bought her son a brand-new Nintendo. We had the Atari for almost a week, but then Mila took it away and gave it to her own children, without even telling us. I missed playing Frogger.

One day while we were watching *ThunderCats*, Santa Claus appeared on the screen during one of the commercial breaks. Christmas was three weeks away, and we'd worried because we didn't have any money to get Papi a present. He only gave us a dollar once in a while. As soon as we'd get it, we'd run down to Barney's Liquors on Monte Vista Street and buy Now & Laters. Sometimes when he was in a good mood, Papi would give us a dollar each, and we'd pool our money and buy a ham-and-cheese sandwich from Fidel's Pizza.

Santa Claus said something I couldn't quite understand. But a telephone number flashed on the screen.

Mago rushed to the rotary phone.

"What are you doing?" Carlos said.

"I'm calling Santa."

"I thought Santa doesn't exist," Carlos said.

"What do you mean he doesn't exist?" I asked. "Don't you see him there on the TV?"

Mago punched Carlos on the arm. "This is the United States, dummy. Everything exists here."

Mago dialed the number and called Santa. She frowned.

"What's wrong?" Carlos said.

"It's in English," Mago said.

"Doesn't Santa speak Spanish?" I asked.

"Shh," Mago said. She listened intently, her eyebrows pulling together as she concentrated. Then she smiled.

"Is it really Santa?" I asked.

"It must be," Mago replied, covering the receiver. "He's talking too fast. All I understood was 'Ho, ho, ho.' It must be him, right?" She told me to be quiet and got back on the line. "Alo? Santa Clos? I want Barbie. I want bike. Please. Me good girl. Tank you." She gave the phone to Carlos.

"Alo? Alo?" Carlos said, smiling his crooked smile. "A Nintendo. A Nintendo to me. Please."

"My turn, my turn!" I said, jumping excitedly. *Wait,*

178

but I don't know how to say "roller skates" in English! I turned to Mago and asked her. Carlos gave me the phone, and I clutched it tightly in my hands. "Come on. He's going to hang up!"

"I don't know, Nena," she said.

Frustrated, I put the phone to my ear. "Alo? Santa Clos? Yo quiero patines. Mándeme unos patines para la Navidad. Tank you." Mago took the phone away and hung up. "Do you think he understood what I said?" I asked them.

"He's Santa Claus. I don't see why not," Mago said. "Don't worry, Nena."

We turned back to the TV, but I was no longer interested in *ThunderCats*. I thought about my skates. In Iguala nobody I knew had skates. You can't skate on dirt roads. But here, oh, this was the perfect place to own skates! But now I'd ruined my chance of getting them because I was sure Santa Claus hadn't understood a word I'd said.

"I can't believe you asked for a Barbie," Carlos teased Mago. She punched him in the arm but didn't say anything. Instead she blushed. I knew why she'd done it. When Papi had bought me a Barbie, Mago had wanted one also, but Papi had said she was too old. He didn't understand that we'd never owned a Barbie, and Mago had yearned for one all her life.

"What are we going to do about a present?" Carlos asked. Christmas was the next day, and we still didn't have anything for Papi. I looked at the Christmas tree Mila had bought at Pic 'n' Save. It wasn't a real tree, but it was the most beautiful tree we'd ever owned. I thought about the branch Tío Crece had painted back in Mexico. Even though we'd done a good job decorating it, nothing could compare to this six-foot-tall beauty shining with colorful lights and glittering with silver garlands.

Mila sent us to buy a bottle of Mazola oil. As we neared the store, Mago stopped and said, "We're going to do something we have never done before. But at this point we have no choice."

"What?" Carlos and I asked. Then Mago shared her plan. Back in Mexico we'd stolen fruit from people's property, but we'd never stolen anything from a store. Barney's Liquors had mirrors on the walls, and the Koreans who owned it never took their eyes off the customers. I'd been there enough times to know that.

"What if we get caught?" I asked, already thinking about the spanking we'd get.

"We won't," Mago said as she pulled us into the store. We split up. Mago would distract the owner while Carlos and I took whatever we thought made good gifts. The thing was that I wished we'd discussed what exactly a *good* gift was. The store didn't have much. As I walked around, my stomach churned from fear of getting caught. The Korean lady kept looking at us. Our image was reflected in the mirrors up above. Luckily, her husband wasn't there, and she couldn't keep her

180

eyes on all three of us, could she? Could she tell we were up to no good?

Nothing seemed good enough for Papi. Canned food, laundry items, diapers, sanitary napkins, toilet paper, soda bottles, chips. *What do I take, what do I take?* I glanced at Carlos. He was by the front looking at the bottles of tequila displayed behind the counter. *What does he think he is doing? He can't reach those bottles!*

Mago picked up the bottle of Mazola oil and took it to the counter. There she knocked over the newspaper rack, and the Korean lady yelled at Mago and hurried to pick up the newspapers. I didn't waste any time. I grabbed an item and hurried out of the store. Carlos came out next, and Mago last. We rushed up Avenue 50 as fast as we could, our hearts beating fast and hard. If we got caught, we'd be deported by Papi!

"So what did you guys get?" Mago asked as we neared the house.

Carlos took a can of Aqua Net hair spray from under his shirt. "They didn't have much to choose from," he said when Mago laughed.

"And you?" she asked.

I showed her what I'd grabbed, a bottle of Tres Flores brilliantine.

"When have you seen Papi wear hair polish?" she asked.

"Never," I said. "But Tío Crece uses it. And so does Tía Güera's husband."

Mago groaned.

181

"It was the only thing for men I could see!" I said, defending myself.

"I can't believe you guys," Mago said as we turned the corner. "We went through all this trouble for those lousy gifts?"

The next day we ended up giving the bottle of brilliantine to Papi and the hair spray to Mila, since we knew for sure she'd use it. Their presents for us were much better, although they weren't what we'd asked Santa for. I got a pair of new Pro Wings tennis shoes. Mago got a pretty peach dress, and Carlos a yellow Tonka truck.

Santa never came. I kept waking up at night and looking at the fireplace by our sofa bed. I wondered if he was running late. He did have many deliveries to make, so was that what was taking so long? But what if he knew we'd stolen from the store? What if he'd decided we weren't good kids and didn't deserve his presents?

Two weeks later Papi called us over to the kitchen, where he and Mila were going through the mail. "What's this?" Papi said, holding a bill in his hand. "Who in the world did you call? Why is the bill so high?"

Mago, Carlos, and I looked at each other. We never used the phone. We didn't know anyone in the U.S., so who would we call?

"We haven't called anyone," Mago said.

"Are you sure?" Mila said.

"Well, a few weeks ago we did call Santa," Mago confessed.

"You did what?" Mila said, taking the bill from Papi to look at the number.

"He was on TV, and he said to call him," Carlos said.

"And we asked him for things, but he didn't bring them," I said.

"I can't believe you kids!" Papi yelled, standing up. We took a step back.

"We didn't know we would get charged for the call," Mago said. "We're sorry, Papi."

"And he didn't *bring* them," I said again.

"I'm still not done paying my friends back the money they let me borrow for the smuggler," Papi said, one hand on his belt buckle. "Otherwise I would put you all on the bus back to Mexico this very night!" He took off his belt and gave us a few lashes with it before grabbing his keys and storming out of the house.

"Don't ever do that again," Mila said, writing out a check and putting it inside the return envelope. "Those are just actors trying to make money."

"We're sorry, Mila," we said, wiping our teary eyes and massaging the stings on our arms from Papi's belt.

Papi returned half an hour later and headed straight to the phone. He worked on it for a few minutes, and we didn't know what he was doing until he was done. "There, now you can't call anymore." We walked up to the phone

183

and saw a lock on it, so now we couldn't turn the little wheel anymore to dial unless we put in a key.

"What if there's an emergency?" Mago asked. "How are we going to call you?"

But Papi was unmoved.

6

After the holidays the girls in fifth and sixth grade were taken to the auditorium for a presentation about menstruation. The girls around me kept giggling as we watched a video, but I didn't. I couldn't understand the words much, but I could understand the images on the screen just fine. Besides, I already knew about menstruation because Mago had told me all about it back in Iguala.

Mago still hadn't become a señorita. Mila said it was because we'd been undernourished in Mexico, which had kept Mago's body from doing what it was supposed to do. Now that we'd been in the U.S. for eight months, and had better food to eat, Mago hoped her period would come soon. I hoped I got mine soon too. Even though I was ten and a half, I couldn't wait to become a señorita.

After the assembly I was given a booklet with a picture of a girl on it. I also got a free sanitary napkin wrapped in cellophane. My very first sanitary napkin! I showed it to Mago as soon as she came home from school.

"Look, look!" I said. "I'm going to become a señorita very soon!" I put my sanitary napkin in my dresser drawer.

Every day after Mago picked me up at Mrs. Giuliano's, I'd rush home and take my sanitary napkin out to look at it. I also tried to read the little booklet I'd gotten. My English still wasn't good. There were many words I didn't yet understand, and I had to keep looking them up in the dictionary. My favorite was "rite of passage." It sounded important.

I was so confused by this sentence: "Changes take place in a girl pretty fast." I couldn't understand why the word "pretty" was there *after* the word "girl." Mr. López had taught me that an adjective goes before the noun, so it should have read "pretty girl." But if that was so, I wondered if only pretty girls got their periods and not ugly ones. I stood in the mirror and looked at myself, wondering which category I was in. I was not pretty like Mago. Even Betty, as little as she was, was prettier than me. Cindy was way prettier than any of us.

"Am I ugly?" I asked Mago.

"Of course not!" she said, but she was my sister, so I knew she had to say that.

The following week Carlos came to pick me up at Mrs. Giuliano's instead of Mago. He said Mago wasn't feeling well and hadn't gone to school. She'd gotten off the bus in front of Burbank, turned around, and gone back home.

When we got home, I did what I always did, opened my drawer to look at my sanitary napkin. But it was gone! I took out the drawer and looked behind the dresser, wondering if it had fallen, but it wasn't there. Mago came out of the bathroom looking very pale.

"What's wrong?" I asked her.

She lay down on the couch, clutching her stomach.

"I have a fever and really bad cramps," she said.

I felt bad for her, but I wanted to know where my sanitary napkin was. I asked her if she'd seen it. "I'm sorry, Nena," she said. "I took it."

"But why?" I yelled. "That was my pad. It was mine!"

"It's just that I got my period this morning, Nena. I couldn't find any pads here, so I didn't know what else to do."

"I hate you!" I yelled, and then I ran outside to the yard to cry.

When Papi came home, he already knew Mago had missed school because he'd gotten a call from Burbank at work. I'd never seen him so furious. He came barging into the house, and without asking for an explanation, he took off his belt and gave my sister the biggest lashing ever, right there on the couch where she'd been writhing in pain all day.

"Papi, stop!" Carlos said, but Papi didn't listen and the belt kept whistling through the air. What was worse was that Mago wouldn't tell him what was wrong with

187

her. She just put her arms up to cover her face. Suddenly I couldn't take it anymore. I forgot I was supposed to be angry at my sister, and I rushed at him and pushed Papi as hard as I could.

"Don't hit her!" I yelled. "She's menstruating. She's become a señorita. Stop it. Stop it!"

Then Papi steadied his belt and put it down. He looked at the three of us, and for a moment it was as if he'd just woken up, as if that person who'd just been beating my sister wasn't the one who was now in the room with us. He blinked once, twice, and then went into his room and didn't come out.

Mila arrived half an hour later. She'd stopped after work to visit her children. When we told her what Papi had done, she said, "Your father didn't mean to. He doesn't know any better. It's the way he was raised." She went to the store to buy Mago a package of sanitary napkins.

I clutched my sister's hand and looked at the angry welts. "Why didn't you tell him?"

"I was too embarrassed, Nena. You just don't go telling men you're on your period. Especially a father you haven't seen in eight years!"

"But he wouldn't have hit you," I said.

Mago looked out the window. "It doesn't matter," she said.

"Of course it matters," Carlos said. "And I can't believe he beat *you* so hard. I mean, you are his favorite."

188

Hearing that, Mago started to cry. I punched Carlos in the arm, even though I was thinking the same thing. Mago was Papi's "Negra," after all.

When Mila came back with the sanitary napkins, Mago took one out of the bag and gave it to me.

"Here, Nena. I know it isn't your special one. I'm sorry."

"It's okay. It was just a pad," I told her. "This one will be just as special to me." I put it in my drawer to save it for the day when I became a little woman. I looked at my father's bedroom door and hoped my rite of passage wouldn't be as painful as my sister's.

7

One day after lunch Mrs. Anderson said the school nurse would be coming in shortly to check the students for hygiene problems. I was surprised at that. Everyone around me looked clean and healthy. All the students had nice clothes on, shoes that were almost new. Nobody was barefoot. No one looked as if they hadn't bathed in days. *Why would we need to be inspected?*

When the nurse came, we formed a single file. I kept my head down while the nurse parted my hair with a wooden stick. When she was done inspecting me, she wrote down something on a paper and said, "You can't return to school until the lice are gone."

"Lice? What lice? No, you're wrong. I can't have lice!" I told her, shaking my head.

As my eyes began to water, I wanted to tell the nurse that I'd been in the U.S. long enough to know that my hygiene problems were a thing of the past. Back in Mexico, I wanted to say, my head had been a nesting ground for lice, my stomach home to tapeworm. Three times a week Abuelita Chinta would send us to the canal to bathe in its muddy waters, and I often went around barefoot. But here in El Otro Lado, I had tennis shoes. I showered almost every day, and the water that sprinkled down from the showerhead was so clean that I could lift up my head, stick out my tongue, and catch the water drops that tasted of rain. We no longer had to wash our clothes in the dirty canal water, nor scrape our knuckles raw from scrubbing our dresses on the washing stones. And we didn't have to lay our wet clothes over rocks until they were hard and stiffened by the sun, which left them smelling and feeling like cardboard.

No, here in the U.S. we went to the Laundromat down the street, where we didn't have to do anything but load the clothes and then sit on a bench and listen to the machine hum and vibrate as it did the work for us. Then off the clothes went into the dryer, where I stood and watched them spin around and around in colorful circles. When the dryer beeped, I opened the door, and the clothes tumbled out into my arms, soft and warm and smelling of flowers, sky, and sunshine. How amazing, I wanted to tell the nurse, that this was how clothes smelled even though they hadn't been touched by a single ray of the sun!

I'd never been so clean in my life, and yet here she was telling me I had lice!

How can there be lice in the U.S.? Did they sneak across the border, like me?

I walked home holding the nurse's note, wondering

what to do. What would Papi say when he found out I couldn't return to class until he took care of the lice problem? What if he finally did decide to send me back to Mexico—never mind that he still hadn't finished paying his debt—after learning that I was still the dirty girl he'd once left behind?

I spent the afternoon crying. I imagined Papi putting me on a bus to Mexico, me waving good-bye to Mago and Carlos from the window. I didn't think I could live without them. And how could I ever hope to make Papi proud of me, when I came home with news such as this?

When Papi got home, I forced myself to walk up to him and give him the note. I stared at the hand in which he held the note. One of his fingernails had dried blood in it, and I wondered if he'd hit himself with a hammer. I wanted to touch his hand, ask him if it hurt. Instead I wrapped my arms around myself, preparing for the beating that I was sure was coming. But I was ready to take as many beatings as he wanted to give me, as long as he didn't send me away. "I'm sorry, Papi," I said. "I don't know how I got lice."

"From other kids at school, I'm sure," he said, hanging up his keys. "It's not your fault."

"You mean, you aren't going to hit me?" I asked.

"Just be careful who you're friends with, Chata. Maybe one of them gave you lice," he said. To my surprise, Papi wasn't angry with me. Instead he spent the rest of the afternoon parting my hair and looking for lice, removing the white nits very carefully so as to not pull out the hair strands. My father, the one who inflicted pain with his belt or his words, the one who had shown little tenderness toward us, who had hands hardened and calloused from so many years of tough manual labor, was very gentle when delousing my hair. How surprised I was that Papi didn't hurt me the way I'd always gotten hurt in Mexico when getting my hair deloused. For the first time since I'd been in this country, Papi devoted a full two hours to me. Only me.

"You probably don't remember this," Papi said as he parted my hair with his fingers. "But when you were little, you used to like it when I gave you baths. You wouldn't let anyone bathe you except me. When I came home for lunch, you would be standing by the door, and as soon as you saw me, you would come running out to me wanting me to bathe you. Sometimes I didn't even have time to eat my lunch. But you wouldn't have it any other way."

I closed my eyes and listened to his story, listened to an event in my life that I didn't remember but that I knew I'd always treasure from that moment on.

8

Even before becoming a señorita, Mago had been changing in many ways. In the past months I'd seen the way she looked at boys whenever we went with Mila on her errands to the market, the Laundromat, or other places. Papi was very clear about that, though. No boyfriends allowed. The month before, Mago had asked him to buy her a makeup set, but Papi had been very clear on that also—she could only wear lipstick. He thought she was too old for Barbies but too young for makeup. Mago said his backward thinking was very frustrating. "This is the United States," she said, "not Mexico."

On Valentine's Day I returned to school free of lice, and just in time to exchange cards with my classmates. I got lots of good candy. Mago and Carlos didn't get anything because junior high students don't exchange Valentine Day cards like kids do in elementary school. Mago said, "We're beyond that nonsense," while popping one of my chocolate hearts into her mouth. I told her that was too bad, and I took away my goodies.

At night, as we were lying in our sofa bed, Mago said, "I'm going on fifteen and I haven't ever been kissed."

"It's not a big deal," I said.

"You're not even eleven. What do you know? I want someone to like me. I want a boyfriend."

"You're not allowed."

"And what if no one ever loves me? What if my scars gross them out?"

"You can hardly see them."

"That's what you think."

"I hope Papi throws you a Quinceañera," I said as I wrapped my arms around her. "You'd look like a princess with your pink dress."

Mago didn't say anything for a while. I thought she was asleep, but then she said, "There's a boy."

I turned to face her again. "Don't tell me you have a boyfriend?" I asked, a little too loudly. Mago hit me with her elbow to be quiet. Carlos didn't wake up, even though he was sleeping on the floor near our bed. I hoped Papi hadn't heard me.

"No. He doesn't even know I exist," she said. She told me about a guy she had a crush on named Pepe. But he didn't even notice her, especially because she was an ESL student. He was a "pocho." Even though his parents were Mexican, he'd been born in this country and didn't speak a word of Spanish. He hung out with the popular kids, unlike Mago, who, because she was an English learner, did not.

195

"Have you tried talking to him?" I asked.

"Are you stupid? He doesn't speak Spanish. Didn't you hear me?"

"Speak to him in English, then."

"My English isn't good enough. It'll never be good enough," she said.

On Monday at school I kept wondering if Mago had any luck with Pepe. When she finally picked me up at Mrs. Giuliano's house, I demanded that she tell me, tell me, tell me!

Mago said, "When Carlos and I were walking down to the bus stop today after school, Pepe and his friends were walking right in front of us. Pepe turned around and saw me. He slowed down until I caught up to him and asked me what my name was."

"And, and?" I said, grabbing her arm. I closed my eyes and listened to her story, which was better than any soap opera.

"All I managed to say was 'Maggie,'" she said. Maggie? It took me a second to remember she'd changed her name at school because her teachers had trouble saying her real name, Magloria, and her history teacher had started calling her Maggie. So now she was known as Maggie everywhere but at home. To me she was still my Mago.

She continued her story: "After I told him my name, Pepe asked me more questions, and very soon he figured out I don't speak English well. He caught up to his friends and didn't look at me again."

"I'm sorry, Mago," I said.

"I could *understand* his questions," she said, close to tears. "I just couldn't answer them. And I was so nervous."

"Don't worry. I'm sure he'll talk to you again. You'll see. You'll get another chance to make a good impression."

But a few days later Mago told me she and Carlos had been walking home again, this time by the train tracks by Figueroa Street, where they ran into Pepe and his friends. To Mago's surprise the boys started throwing gravel at them from the other side of the tracks, yelling, "Wetbacks! Wetbacks!"

Mago told me her heart broke at seeing Pepe laughing and pointing at her and Carlos. "You don't know how much I wished today that I knew every bad word in English," Mago said between sobs. "And there was no point in cussing them out in Spanish. They wouldn't have understood the words. And worse, they would have laughed even harder."

Mago wasn't the only one who was in love. A few days later when she and Carlos came home from school, I found out about a girl named María who Carlos had been crushing on. Now he was very upset about something that happened on the bus, and he and Mago were still arguing about it.

"You didn't have to be so mean to her," Carlos told Mago.

"What happened?" I asked.

Carlos said, "There's a girl named María I like a lot. Her last name is González, so I get to sit behind her in the three classes we share."

"But she doesn't even know he exists," Mago said. He looked away, and his cheeks turned red. I knew Carlos didn't have much luck with girls because of his crooked teeth, which was really sad, because my brother wasn't ugly. But once he opened his mouth and you could see his teeth, well, then that was *all* you looked at.

"You should have seen him today on the bus," Mago said as she dropped down onto the couch. "There he is, staring at María from across the aisle, drooling like a cow. It was embarrassing. And finally this girl comes up to him, really angry, and says, 'What are you staring at me for?'"

"And you didn't have to be so mean!" Carlos said again.

"What did you tell her?" I asked Mago as I sat next to her.

"Well, what else? I said, 'You should be grateful my brother is looking at you. You're so ugly.'"

"And she's not!" Carlos said.

"I was trying to defend you, dummy," Mago said. We all jumped up from the couch when the doorbell suddenly rang.

Carlos opened the door. He turned to look at us, his eyes opened wide in shock.

198

"Tell your sister to come out," a girl said in Spanish through the screen door.

"It's *her*," Carlos said. "How did she know where we lived?"

"How would I know?" Mago said, heading to the door. "What do you want, girl? You want my brother to stare at you some more?"

"I came to kick your butt," the girl said.

"Okay, give me a minute." Mago headed to our dresser and took out a pair of sweatpants and a sweatshirt. She went into the bathroom and changed out of her jeans and blouse.

"Mago, don't go outside," Carlos pleaded. "I don't need you to defend me. I'm not a little kid anymore."

"This is no longer about you," she said as she bent down to retie her tennis shoes.

I walked over to the door, and there I saw the girl who my brother had been drooling over like a cow. Behind her were three other girls. María was very pretty. Her skin was light and she had a few freckles sprinkled on her cheeks. She was wearing white jeans, a black Hello Kitty shirt, and white sandals. I instantly envied her Hello Kitty shirt. It'd been almost a year since Mila had taken us to Kmart to buy us clothes. She'd been bringing us bags of clothes from the old ladies at the retirement home where she worked. Mago said those were dead people's clothes. I didn't know if the old ladies were dead or not. All I knew was that

199

there was no way I'd ever find a Hello Kitty shirt in the bags Mila brought us.

I wanted to hate this girl María, but I felt it wasn't fair to hate her simply because I wanted her shirt.

I wanted to tell the girl she needed to go home. But too soon Mago was pushing me out of the way and heading to the six-car parking lot because it was almost empty right now.

"Look, I'm sorry, María. I won't look at you again, but you don't need to fight my sister," Carlos said.

María pushed him aside and called him a sissy. She and her friends followed Mago to the parking lot.

María didn't know that Carlos wasn't trying to protect Mago. She didn't know that the previous week Mago's heart had been broken, and ever since then she'd been itching to punch something or someone. María didn't know that only the day before, Mago had hit me because I'd taken her rubber band without permission to put my hair up into a ponytail. And she'd punched Carlos in the stomach for spilling water onto her math homework. María soon found out.

A second after they reached the parking lot, the fight broke out, and Mago had her fingers wrapped in María's long brown hair and was punching her as hard as she could. This time Mago didn't hold her cuss words back. María spoke perfect Spanish, so Mago fired off her cuss words faster than a machine gun. Soon she had María on the ground, and the girl's pretty white pants were turning gray. But the worst part came when Mago dragged María to the space where Papi parked the old Ford truck he drove to work. Mago rolled María around and around in the puddle of motor oil from the truck, and soon María's white pants were completely black and her friends were rushing over to pull Mago off.

"Enough, enough!" the girls said as they formed a barricade to protect María.

Mago wiped the sweat off her forehead and looked at the girl lying in the puddle of motor oil. "When my brother looks at you again, you better be happy about it."

Mago walked back to the apartment, and Carlos and I followed behind her. He turned to look one more time at the girl he loved. She was on her feet now, trying to smooth out her messy hair.

Carlos said, "You aren't ugly, María. I am." And then with his head hanging down, he went inside.

I stood there in the parking lot feeling terrified. *What's going to happen to* me *when I fall in love? Will I have the same rotten luck as my brother and sister?* I went back to the apartment thankful that the next day February would be officially over.

9

One day at school Mrs. Anderson announced that there was something important she had to tell us. Aldama Elementary was having a writing competition! That week all the students would be writing our very own books, and the teachers would choose the best books in their classes. From there the selected books would be judged and three lucky winners chosen. I would finally get a chance to make Papi proud!

For the rest of the week we worked on our projects. Mr. López told me and the other immigrant students we could write our stories in Spanish because that was the language we knew best. At first I didn't know what to write. I'd never written my very own story. I had always liked to read in Mexico, but here in this country the books for kids my age were very difficult for me to read in English. The only books I could read were for kindergartners! Books with big letters and lots of pictures. I loved looking at the pictures, but the stories weren't very interesting.

I thought and thought about what to write, and finally I knew—the story of my birth.

As I wrote, I closed my eyes and pictured Mami lying down on the straw mat on the dirt floor. I saw the midwife coming into the shack where Mami was bending over in pain. The midwife lit a fire and put a pot of water on to boil. As I wrote, I could really feel that I was there. I could even feel the heat of the flames.

"Don't push yet," I heard the midwife say as she sharpened her knife. "You aren't ready yet."

I wrote that I couldn't wait to be born and the midwife barely had enough time to catch me before I hit the dirt floor. "It's a girl," I heard the midwife say as she put me into Mami's arms.

Then came the best part of my story, my favorite part. Mami turned to face the fire so that the heat of the flames could warm me. As the midwife cut the umbilical cord, Mami suddenly pointed to a spot on the dirt floor and told the midwife to bury the umbilical cord there. I wrote that even though I was now living far away from Mami and my country, I hadn't forgotten where I came from.

Mr. López helped me fix my spelling and gave me suggestions for improving my story. When it was as good as could be, he gave me white paper to copy it onto neatly. When I finished, I started my favorite part, drawing pictures.

Mrs. Anderson showed the class how to bind our

books. She gave us two rectangular pieces of cardboard and butcher paper to make the cover. By the end of the week we were all done with our books, and Mrs. Anderson collected them and put them in piles at her desk. Because it was now Friday, and we'd worked hard all week, she put on a movie for us to watch as a reward. She'd read our books while we watched our movie.

The movie was about an alien named E.T. who wanted to go home. I felt bad for the alien because life in the U.S. was very difficult for him. I could understand his wanting to go home. I was also jealous because E.T. learned English a lot faster than me!

I couldn't concentrate on the movie. I kept glancing at Mrs. Anderson. She put all the books on the right side of her desk. Then as she read, she made two other piles, one for the books she liked, and the other pile for the ones she didn't. One pile was getting bigger and bigger, and the other pile remained small. I knew the big pile was of the books she hadn't liked.

I froze when she picked up my book. *Here it is. Here is my big chance!* She opened it and flipped through the pages in the blink of an eye. Then she closed the book shut and put it in the big pile. My eyes began to burn with tears. My book was rejected! *But she couldn't have read it. No one reads a book in a second! She doesn't even speak Spanish well, so how could she read it so fast?* I wanted to stand up and say something. I wanted to tell her she'd made a mistake and she must look at it again, but I didn't have the English words to say what I thought—how I felt—so I said nothing at all.

E.T. was going home. He was saying bye to his friend and getting into his ship. How I wished I could go home too, back to Iguala, where I could speak to my teacher in my own language. Where I could stand up for what I believed in, not caring if afterward I'd get hit with the ruler for my rebellion. I didn't want to be in this country if that was how things were going to be.

At the end of class, Mrs. Anderson held up the books she had chosen for the competition. Out of the eight books she'd picked, not even one had been written by the kids at my table, the non-English speakers.

"You kids did a great job on those books," Mr. López said to us in Spanish. "Just because they weren't chosen doesn't mean they aren't good."

"Just not good enough," I said under my breath. I put my head between my hands, tears threatening to come out as I felt the disappointment come at me like a huge wave. *Don't let go of me, Papi.*

Mr. López looked at me, and then at the other four students at my table. He said, "There's no reason for any of you not to get ahead in life. You will learn English one day. You'll find your way. Remember, it doesn't matter where you come from. You're now living in the land of opportunity, where anything is possible."

Mrs. Anderson put all the rejected books around the room to display them. I knew she was doing that so the students wouldn't feel bad for not being chosen. But when we were dismissed, as I was walking by my book, I took it from the shelf where Mrs. Anderson had put it.

One day, I promised myself, thinking about Mr. López's words, *I will write a book that won't be rejected, one that will make my father proud.*

10

"Your mother isn't in Mexico," Papi said to us one day after he got back from downtown LA. He opened a beer and took a long sip from it but didn't take his eyes off us.

We stared at him, not understanding.

"Didn't you hear me? Your mother is not in Mexico," Papi said again. I thought he was joking. Then I realized he wasn't.

"Where is she, then?" Mago asked, lifting her head from her homework. Carlos and I also stopped writing and sat there at the kitchen table looking at our father.

"She's been in this country for months now, and she hasn't even tried to contact you kids," Papi said.

"But how can she be here?" Carlos asked.

"Are you sure?" I asked.

"Of course I'm sure," Papi said. "I ran into her today." He told us that on his way back home from downtown, he'd waited for the bus. When it had pulled over, to his surprise the last passenger to get off was our mother! She lived downtown on a street called San Pedro.

"Your mother never ceases to amaze me," Papi said.

"And Betty?" Mago asked.

"Didn't I just tell you? Your mother amazes me. Where do you think your little sister is?"

Mago, Carlos, and I looked at one another. *Where else could Betty be? With Mami, of course.*

"Your mother," Papi said, squeezing the empty beer can with his hand, "your mother left your sister in Mexico and came here with her boyfriend." He threw the can against the wall and grabbed another one.

"Can we go see her?" Carlos asked.

"Did she tell you where exactly she lives?" Mago asked.

"You want to go *see* her?" Papi said. "Don't you kids have any pride? Your mother doesn't care about you. If she did, she would have contacted you when she got here. She's been here for months. Months. Why would you want to go see her? Have some pride!"

"But she's our mami," I said.

Papi looked at me, and I could tell in his eyes that I'd disappointed him with those words. He shook his head and left. At the door he turned and looked at us again. "Just so you know, your mother has a new child. A boy, not three months old."

I felt something squeezing my chest, and I couldn't breathe, I couldn't think. All I heard in my head were Papi's words: *Your mother doesn't care about you. . . . Your mother doesn't care about you. . . .*

But even when the dizziness stopped and I could

208

breathe again, I found that I couldn't stop myself from wanting to see my mother.

For the next few weeks after Papi's discovery, we couldn't convince him to allow us to go see Mami. He simply said, "I'm the one who brought you here," and then locked himself up in his room. With those words, he was asking us to choose between him and her. We didn't know how to tell him it shouldn't be a matter of choice. They were both our parents!

It hurt me to think of Betty all alone in Mexico. When Papi and Mami had left us there, at least we'd had one another. But Betty, who did Betty have over there? She was like Élida, with no one there to love her except our grandmother. I thought about all those Polaroid pictures we'd sent, of how it must have hurt our little sister to see us here, together, while she was all alone.

"Your mother is so selfish, that's why she wouldn't let me bring Betty," Papi said to us. "She used your sister to get back at me."

"We couldn't afford another mouth to feed, anyway," Mila told him. "It's difficult enough as it is, with the three you already have here. With the three I have. Even though they aren't with me, I still have to support them."

"Yes, but what if I went back—"

"We're not going through that again," Mila said. "I will not take responsibility for raising yet another child!"

209

Mago wrote a letter to Abuelita Chinta, and we waited anxiously for a reply. It wasn't until the end of June that a letter came from my aunt, Tía Güera. She told us our little sister was fine and not to worry. She gave us great news. Later in the summer she'd leave Iguala to come here to the U.S. and would bring Betty along. The only bad thing was, Tía Güera wrote, that she'd have to leave her own daughter, Lupita, behind with my grandmother. It made me sad to think of my cousin Lupita being abandoned, and I hoped one day the cycle of leaving children behind would end.

We finally convinced Papi to let us visit Mami when we heard that Tía Güera and Betty had safely arrived from Mexico.

We took the 83 bus to downtown Los Angeles. As we walked east on 7th Street toward San Pedro Street, we were shocked by what we saw. Here was a side to this country I hadn't seen before. For a moment I felt as if we'd just crossed over into another world.

There were homeless people sitting on the ground asking for spare change. Some were pushing shopping carts filled with everything they owned. Trash littered the sidewalks. Plastic bags whirled up in the air like miniature parachutes. The stench of urine made me gag.

We looked at each other. How could this be where Mami lived?

"If I didn't know any better, I would think we were back in Mexico," Mago said.

"I didn't think there were places like this in the U.S.," Carlos said.

In Iguala everyone I knew always thought of the U.S. as the most beautiful place in the world, as close to heaven as you could possibly get.

We found the address Tía Güera had given us and knocked. A woman came down the stairs and opened the security door. We didn't know who she was, but we told her we were there to see our mother.

"What's her name?" she asked.

"Juana."

"Oh yes, she lives in room A." She went back up the stairs, and we followed behind her. The door to room A was open. We saw Mami before she saw us. She was sitting on the bed holding a sleeping baby in her arms. When she saw us, she stood up and came to the door.

"I can't believe you kids are here," she said, smiling. "Look how much you've grown!"

We entered the room and said hello to Rey, who was sitting at the table. Next to him was Tía Güera. We gave her a hug and told her it was nice to see her. Then my eyes fell on little Betty sitting quietly on the dirty carpet, playing with a doll. We rushed to our sister to hug her and cover her in kisses, but Betty pushed us away and ran to my aunt's side. "A year is a long time for a little kid," Tía Güera said.

"Give her time," Mami said.

"Betty, it's me, Mago. Don't you remember me?" Mago said, kneeling down to look at her. Betty hid her face in Tía Güera's chest and didn't want to talk to us.

I looked at my five-year-old sister and wondered how long it would take for us to finally feel like a family again.

Mami lived in a tiny room big enough for a bed, a dining table, a refrigerator, a TV stand, and boxes of clothes piled against the wall. They had to share the kitchen and bathroom with the rest of the tenants on their floor. I thought about the fourplex Mila and Papi owned. They didn't make much money, and between Mila and Papi, they had six kids to support. Their many expenses didn't allow them to afford the rent of the larger units. We had to stay in the one-bedroom unit until things got better. But even though we slept in the living room, we at least had the bathroom and kitchen to ourselves, and we didn't have to share them with complete strangers. We also had a backyard to play in. Our carpet wasn't dirty. There weren't roaches scurrying around the walls like there were here at my mother's.

We crammed into the little room as best we could.

"So how did you end up here?" we asked Mami.

She sat at the table holding her sleeping son in her arms. I tried not to look at him. I didn't want to feel anything for this baby, this brother of mine whose name was Leonardo. Even though he was three months old, he looked just like his father. Mago, Carlos, Betty, and

I looked like Mami and Papi, and anyone who saw us could tell right away that we were siblings. But Leonardo looked nothing like us.

Mami told us her journey to the U.S. with Rey happened by chance. "My friend's son wanted to come here, but he was afraid of coming alone," she said. "So my friend offered to lend me money so Rey and I could come and keep her son company during the border crossing."

Except she couldn't bring Betty, so she had left her behind with Abuelita Chinta until she got settled here. In the meantime she'd started another family with Rey—a boy we wouldn't have known about if Papi hadn't run into her that day.

Both Rey and Mami worked at a garment factory. "They pay us miserable wages," Mami said. "As you can tell by where we live." A roach scurried across the wall, and she hurried to squash it with her sandal. She turned to us and said, "But no poverty here can compare to the poverty we left behind. And at least now I'm closer to you, my children."

Mago asked her the question we'd been dying to ask. "Why didn't you come see us?"

Mami took a deep breath and said, "I wanted to give you kids a chance to get to know your father, and for him to know you, without me coming in between you. Do you understand?"

Strangely enough, we did understand, but we didn't believe that was the only reason. I finally realized there wasn't much room for us in our mother's life. She'd never be able to love us the way we wanted to be loved by her—with all her heart, the way a mother should love. But we wanted her in our lives, no matter how little of herself she was able to give us.

We began to visit her every other Sunday. Despite the measly salary Mami earned at the factory, she always had enough money to take us out, like to Exposition Park to see the roses, to the Alley to buy us underwear or socks, to Placita Olvera to see the folklórico dances and have a churro.

What I didn't like was that whenever we went out with Mami, she would bring a plastic bag and pick up cans from the street or look through trash bins. Sometimes she even made us pick up the cans for her, even in public places. It was so embarrassing for Mago, Carlos, and me that we soon started to say no, absolutely not! Betty, who didn't know any better, ended up being the one to run around picking up the cans without Mami even having to ask her to do it. She would run back to Mami with her find, laughing while beer trickled down her bare arm.

"What do you do with those cans?" Carlos asked. We'd seen homeless people around her apartment building pushing carts filled with cans on their way to someplace, but we had no idea where they took them.

"I take them to the recycling center," Mami said. "I get good money doing this." Good money or not, Mami's apartment always smelled like rotten beer and soda because she only went to the recycling center once a week, so the bags of smashed cans just sat in a corner of her apartment all week long. Now I knew why there were so many roaches.

Eventually we became used to our double lives. Yet as the months went by, I still wished there was a way we could have both our parents together, in the same place. I especially wished this when I graduated from Aldama Elementary a year later. Although I was happy to see Papi, who actually took time off work to come to my graduation, I wished Mami was there too. But that was where Papi had drawn the line. He didn't want to see Mami. He said he'd never forgive her for what she'd done to Betty.

Mami didn't ask much about him, either. She embraced her new life in this country with Rey and her new baby boy and Betty. We weren't separated by two thousand miles anymore, but it still felt as if a huge distance existed between us.

11

Sometimes Papi would sit us down and talk and talk as if trying to make up for the eight years he was gone from our lives. But his talks were always about the future, and they always went like this:

"Here in this country if you aren't educated, you won't go very far."

"School is the key to the future."

"You kids have to study hard. You hear me?"

He told us how important it was to get an education so that one day we could have a good career. "For example, look at your mother," he said. "What's she doing at a factory? That's a dead-end job. You get paid cash, don't get benefits. She's not putting money into Social Security for retirement. That's not the way to live, not here in this country." He didn't mention that he wasn't getting much out of his job either, since he was using a Social Security card he'd bought at MacArthur Park for a hundred dollars.

"One day you will have great careers. Be home owners. Have money for retirement," he said.

"But I'm only eleven and a half, Papi," I said. "Why do I need to worry about retiring?"

"Chata, one day you will get old," Papi said. "If you think life is hard now, wait until you get so old that you can't even shower on your own. Then you'll really see how hard life is."

"Like the old people at your work?" I asked.

"Yes, but you wouldn't be able to afford Kingsley Manor if you didn't have a good job before you got too old to work," Papi said. "But see, if you plan ahead, then you will be better off."

"But we don't have papers, Papi," Mago said. "How are we going to be home owners or have good careers with no papers?"

Papi said, "Just because we're undocumented doesn't mean we can't dream. Besides," he said, "our lives are going to change for the better. Soon that will no longer be an issue."

Papi had been looking at ways to legalize our status. He and Mila got officially married so she could use her privileges as an American citizen to apply for our green cards. Also, ever since President Reagan had approved an amnesty bill eight months before, in November of 1986, Papi had been going through the application process and was hoping to get his green card through that program. Once he did, he could then claim us and legalize our status if our applications through Mila didn't work out.

"One way or another," Papi said, "we will stop living in the shadows."

I didn't know what exactly he meant by that, but when I thought about the way Mrs. Anderson ignored me, about the fact that I couldn't express myself in class, and that my lack of English kept me silent, I thought I understood what Papi meant.

In September, Mago became the first person in our family to attend high school. Papi took her shopping for new school clothes, saying that his "Negra" needed to look her best on such an important day, because after this she was going to go on to college and make us all proud.

"How about me?" I asked. "I need clothes too. I'm starting junior high."

"But you weren't the first one," Mago said. "I was."

Papi told me and Carlos that he didn't have enough money for us all. His salary as a maintenance worker didn't go very far to support his three children, and paying lawyer fees and the fees for our green card applications had gotten us more into debt. I wished I understood all that, and I tried, but when Papi and Mago left for Fashion 21, I was left behind, angry at my father for not taking Carlos and me clothes shopping as well.

I was also angry at my sister. It wasn't my fault she was the firstborn. It wasn't my fault she got to do everything before I did. Papi said he wanted us to stop living in the shadows. Whether we got green cards or not, I promised myself I would stop living in the shadow of my sister. I would find a way to be the first at something. Something that would make my father proud.

I had thought Aldama Elementary was big, but I was overwhelmed when I saw that Burbank Junior High School was even bigger. Thankfully, I wouldn't be there alone. Carlos was starting ninth grade, and he'd be there with me for a year. He took me to my first class, which was Intermediate ESL. Finally I'd no longer be in a corner of my classroom as I learned English. I'd be in a room where the whole class was composed of English learners.

My teacher's name was Mr. Salazar. His name sounded familiar, and I couldn't remember where I'd heard it until he took roll. When he called out my name, he paused and asked, "Grande? Are you by any chance related to Maggie Grande?"

"Yes, she's my sister," I said, remembering that Mago had mentioned him to me before.

Mr. Salazar had a huge thick mustache, but even his bushy whiskers couldn't cover up that big smile. "Your sister was a wonderful student. She was one of my best and brightest." He looked at me, as if measuring me up. My stomach churned. I just knew that no matter what I did, he'd always compare me to my sister. And even if I did end up being one of his "best and brightest," Mago had done it first.

Luckily, no one knew my sister in my math and science

219

classes, so there was a chance I could prove myself there without being compared to Mago, although those were my least favorite subjects. In PE, as the teacher took roll, she stopped at my name, and once again my stomach made a flip. "Reyna Grande?" she asked. "Is that really your name, Reyna *Grande*?"

I tried to ignore the students' giggles. *Yeah, yeah, I'm a big queen but I'm only four foot eight inches tall, so what?*

"Yes, that's me," I said, already thinking she was going to ask me if I was Mago's sister. But I was surprised when she didn't.

"You're too young to be called that, don't you think?" she asked with a smile. Her hair was so blond, it was almost white under the sunlight. "Do you mind if I call you Princess?"

I was so relieved that she didn't know my sister, I almost shouted out a big yes! I agreed with her that I was too young to be called Big Queen. Maybe one day I would grow into my name. For now I was happy being a princess!

My last class was something called band. Carlos said it was an elective, but I hadn't chosen it. All the other electives, besides metal shop and band, had already been taken, so when the counselor had been filling out my schedule, he'd said, "I'll put you in band," without asking me if that was what I wanted. I knew it had something to do with music, but I didn't really know what to expect. Carlos had asked to be put in metal shop.

As I walked into my classroom, I hit my foot on the leg of a chair. I cried out in pain. The teacher asked, "Are you okay?"

I took a deep breath and answered in English as best as I could, "Yes, teacher. I just hurt my big finger." I limped to an empty chair and sat, feeling proud of myself for answering him in his own language.

"Your big finger?" he asked. All the students were looking at me weird. "Oh, you mean your big toe!" he said, and laughed. Everyone else laughed with him.

"You don't have fingers on your feet," he gently explained. "You have toes."

I wanted to slap myself because I should have known that. I'd learned body parts at Aldama. It's just that sometimes I still forgot things like that. In Spanish there is only one word for finger or toe, so you don't have to worry about whether your "dedo" is on your feet or hands. Why did English have to be so complicated?

When the teacher, whose name was Mr. Adams, asked me what instrument I wanted to play, I didn't know what to say. He pointed to the closets, where I saw rows upon rows of black cases. He opened several cases to reveal beautiful golden and silver instruments whose names I did not know.

"So, which one do you want to play?" he asked again.

"How much it costs?" I asked, wondering if Papi would even have any money to buy me one of those instruments. They looked expensive.

Mr. Adams laughed. "They won't cost you a thing," he said. "They belong to the school, but you can borrow them and take them home with you."

I found that completely unbelievable. In Mexico nothing was free in school. Not even a pencil. He asked me again what I wanted to play. I didn't know much about instruments. He told me their names as he pointed to them: clarinet, trumpet, trombone, piccolo, flute, saxophone, French horn. So many instruments that I could take home!

"Here, try this," he said. "You need a small instrument." He handed me a clarinet.

Just then my eyes fell upon the shiny golden beauty in one of the cases. I said, "That's the one I want."

Mr. Adams turned to look where I was pointing. He said, "It's an alto sax. You sure that's the one you want?"

"Yes, I'm sure."

"But you're so small," he said. I reached out my hand, and he gave me the case.

When we all had our instruments, Mr. Adams showed us how to play them and how to read music notes. The saxophone was heavy, and the neck strap dug into my skin. I got dizzy as I blew through the mouthpiece, and at first I couldn't make anything but squeaky noises. By the end of class, I'd managed to create something that sounded like music, and for the first time I felt excited. I loved playing an instrument because it didn't matter whether I spoke perfect English or not. Who cared if I had a "wetback" accent? Reading music didn't require me to be fluent in any language. And I didn't need to speak, just play sweet melodies.

I went home with my alto sax, and as soon as Papi got home, I showed it to him. Mago had never come home with an instrument, so finally I had found something I was first at! Papi held the alto sax in his hands and turned it this way and that way. "Are you sure you don't have to pay for this?" he asked.

"No, Papi. The school lets students borrow them for free."

Papi was amazed. He asked me to play something. Mago rolled her eyes at me and left us alone. I took the sax from him and played the scale Mr. Adams had taught me, except I didn't remember it that well. But Papi didn't criticize me for messing up. He patted my head and told me to keep practicing.

"You know, Chata, when I was in third grade, my teacher brought some drums to class and started to teach us to play them. We couldn't take them home, but still, it was nice coming to school and having the chance to learn to play an instrument."

"I didn't know you could play the drums!" I said.

Papi's smile faded. "I can't," he said. "You see, a few weeks later, when I turned nine, your grandfather said I was old enough to join him at the fields, and he pulled me out of school. I never got to play the drums again. And I've been working ever since."

223

Papi got up and headed to the refrigerator to grab a Budweiser. Then he went to his room. I sat in the living room to practice on the sax, but Mago and Carlos complained about the noise and sent me outside. I went to the yard and continued to practice, and I played with all my heart, for me and for my papi, who never got another chance to play anything.

12

Just like Abuela Evila, Papi didn't allow us to play in the neighborhood. He said, "I want you here, at home, where I can see what you're doing. I won't have you hanging out with the wrong kids and becoming cholos."

We weren't interested in becoming gang members, but it was hard not to come across them. Highland Park was home to one of the biggest gangs in Los Angeles— the Avenues. There was a family of Avenues living next door to us, in fact. Although we tried to stay away from them, they didn't stay away from us. One of the boys, Tino, snuck into our yard every few nights to fill up his buckets with water from the garden hose. Their utilities were always getting shut off because they didn't pay their bills on time. The father was in jail, and the mother was always doing drugs instead of taking care of her children.

Papi ignored them. He said, "I'm not going to put our lives in danger for a bucket of water." But one night, when Papi was coming home from the liquor store with a six-pack of beer, a gang member came out of the shadows with a knife and told Papi to hand over his wallet. In the dim light of the streetlamp, Papi caught a glimpse of the boy's face and said, "I let you take water from me, and now you're threatening me with a knife?"

Papi later told us that Tino had actually apologized to him and put his knife away. "Good thing I've never said anything about the water," Papi said. "He would have stabbed me right there, because I wasn't about to hand over my wallet."

The firing of gunshots was common in our neighborhood. Almost every night we heard popping noises in the distance. But one night we heard three noises right outside our door! Mago, Mila, and I were in the living room watching our favorite soap opera, *Quinceañera*, and we were so engrossed in the TV that we didn't pay much attention. But then Papi and Carlos were running into the house, and Papi was yelling, "Get down. Get down!" We dropped down to the floor right away. Mago didn't take her eyes off the TV, and she was too busy drooling over Ernesto Laguardia to care about what was going on.

"What's happening, Natalio?" Mila asked. It was now quiet outside except for the barking of a dog and a car alarm going off.

Papi had been outside finishing some repairs on the plumbing, and Carlos had been practicing his soccer moves in the parking lot. Papi said a car drove by and shot at three gang members walking by. The bullets shattered the windshield of one of the tenants' cars. Carlos had been playing just a few inches away from that car.

"One of the cholos got hit," Papi said. "He's still out there, but the others took off running."

When we were sure no more gunshots would follow, we went outside. It was dark, and it took us a few seconds to see the man crawling on the sidewalk toward us. "Help me," he said, groaning. "Help me."

Papi stood in front of Mago, Carlos, Mila, and me and put his arms out, keeping us back. We stood still, too horrified to move or make a sound. The young man's head was shaved close to his scalp—a typical sign of a gang member—and he was wearing a plaid long-sleeve shirt. He grabbed hold of the front gate and tried to pull himself up. "Help me," he said again.

I looked at Papi. Why wasn't Papi helping him? "Do something," I pleaded, pulling on his sleeve.

"Let's go inside," Papi said.

"But he'll die," Mago said.

"Go inside," Papi insisted. Mila went straight to the phone and called 911.

"We have to help him!" I pleaded.

"We've done all we can for him," Papi said. "If I go out there and help him, tomorrow I'll be the one who gets shot. Or you kids. That stupid gang will come seeking revenge, believe me. I don't want to come home and find one of you kids clinging to the gate with a bullet hole in your chest!"

227

I recognized the terror in my father's face. I'd seen it once before, at the border, during our third crossing as we'd been running from the helicopter and he'd been trying to protect us.

We stood there in the kitchen looking at each other. Soon we heard sirens approaching the house. Papi went out and told us to stay inside. We looked out the window and saw the police and the ambulance arrive. We were too curious to do as we were told. We'd never seen a shot man before. The three of us went outside just as the paramedics were trying to pry the man's fingers from our gate. They laid him on the sidewalk and tore open his shirt. He wasn't moving or breathing. On the right side of his chest was a small bullet hole. I stared at the pool of blood beneath our gate. I reached to grab my father's hand, and he squeezed it tight.

13

While we waited for our green card applications to be processed, Papi decided to go to adult school and learn English once and for all. So far he had depended on Mila for everything. She had to write out the checks to pay the bills. She had to take me, Mago, and Carlos to our doctors' appointments because Papi didn't feel comfortable doing it. Mila went grocery shopping. Mila went to our parent-teacher conferences because Papi made her go in his place. Mila dealt with their Asian tenants who couldn't speak Spanish. Papi stayed in his room and wouldn't come out, except to go to work or to the liquor store.

But one day Papi bought himself a notebook and borrowed a pencil and a sharpener from me. I even gave him my eraser that smelled of strawberries, for good luck. We watched as he left the house and headed to Franklin High School's night classes for adults. It filled me with pride to see my father go to school. All his talk about education, about the importance of school, seemed to mean so much more when I saw him full of determination to learn.

"Once I'm a legal resident, things are going to change around here," he often said.

My mother had received her legal residency through the Immigration Reform and Control Act of 1986. She'd legalized her status before Papi had, and yet, unlike him, she had no desire to learn English. She had no motivation to change her life just because she was no longer undocumented. But my father's desire for a better life was real. It was contagious. It was one of the things I most respected about him.

Yet, a few weeks after he'd been going to school, Papi found out something terrible.

Tía Emperatriz had stolen his dream house!

My aunt had finally gotten married, and she'd managed to get Abuela Evila to give her all the family property, which included the land on which Papi's house was built, and she'd moved herself and her husband right into my father's dream house.

"How could she do that?" Mila asked. "Your own sister. And your mother, why would she hand over your house to Emperatriz, just like that? You've been a good son. Look at all the money you've been sending her all these years. Without you she would have starved already."

"What are you going to do?" Mago asked Papi. We knew what that house meant to Papi. We knew it was his backup plan in case things didn't work out for him here in the U.S. It was an investment that had cost us our

230

relationship with our parents, that had cost Mami her marriage with my father. The price for that house was too high to pay, as Mami had once said. And now it had been stolen from him.

"I'm going to go over there and get my house back!" Papi said, slamming his fist onto the kitchen table.

"You can't go, Natalio. You'll have to sneak across the border again, and if you get caught, your green card application will not be approved. Do you really want to jeopardize your chance of becoming a legal resident?" Mila said.

But Papi wasn't listening. He paced the kitchen back and forth. He ran his fingers through his hair. Then he stopped pacing and looked at us.

"I'm not going to lose that house. I can't lose that house. It's all I have."

"But we don't have money to pay for your plane ticket. We don't have money to pay for a smuggler to bring you back," Mila insisted. "We're barely making it as it is."

But Papi wouldn't listen, and by the next day he was gone.

While he was in Mexico, it took a lot of effort for me to stay focused in school. I wondered what Papi was doing. I wondered if by now my aunt and my grandmother had realized their mistake and given the house back to its rightful owner. I wondered if he was already on his way back to us. I prayed that he crossed the border safely. I prayed that he didn't get killed or hurt or caught by la migra. My stomach hurt knowing that if he got caught, he'd lose his chance of becoming a legal resident, of finally having that security he desperately wanted. And what would become of his dreams, which were now also my dreams?

Two weeks later we came home from school to find Papi sitting at the kitchen table, his head hanging low. His face was pale, despite the sunburn he'd gotten while running across the border. His eyes were red and puffy from lack of sleep. He looked thinner than he had when he'd left. We rushed to him, happy he'd made it across the border safely. He turned to us and said, "I'm never going back there again."

I thought about all those times that Mago, Carlos, and I had carried bricks and buckets of mortar to the bricklayers. I thought about those nights when we couldn't sleep because we were too sore. I thought about the years Papi was gone, that Mami was gone, so they could build that dream house.

"What happened, Papi?" Mago asked.

He said Abuela Evila was ill and frail, and somehow my aunt had managed to coerce her into giving her the property. While he was there, my aunt said what was done was done. She said Papi didn't need a house when he had so much already. Didn't he live here in this beautiful country? What more could he want? Papi said that neither his father nor his mother stood up for him, that neither parent fought by his side. He said, "I've never felt so alone in my life."

I wished I could go to my father and wrap my arms around him, tell him I understood his loss, tell him that it hurt me as much as it hurt him. He shouldn't feel alone— he had us, his children. But I didn't know how to hold him. I didn't know how to say what I felt, so I said nothing at all.

In the evenings at five thirty, I looked at Papi's bedroom door and wondered if that day would be the day when he'd finally come out with his notebook under his arm, ready to go back to school. But the door stayed closed. After two weeks of looking at his closed door, I realized that the dream house wasn't the only thing he had lost.

14

When eighth grade began, I had two things to celebrate. I had officially become a señorita and had successfully completed the ESL program! Thanks to my addiction to reading, I had learned English well enough to be enrolled in regular English classes starting in the new school year.

Every Friday before heading home, I would stop at Arroyo Seco library and check out ten books. I'd read them all throughout the week. I read so much that sometimes I'd hide under the covers with a flashlight and not go to sleep until I was finished with my book. My favorites were by a writer named V. C. Andrews. Her characters had evil grandmothers, divorced parents, and separated siblings. V. C. Andrews wrote about poverty, sadness, loss, and heartbreaks. I recognized myself in her characters' pain and suffering. I also liked the series Sweet Valley High, about twins named Jessica and Elizabeth who got into all sorts of mischief. They had blond hair and blue-green eyes and lived in a beautiful home with two parents who loved them. The twins lived in the perfect America that I wished I lived in.

Eventually I had to get eyeglasses. Mago said, "Now you look like a librarian," as if to insult me. But it only made me love books even more.

Halfway into the school year, I found out Burbank was having a short-story competition. My English teacher encouraged all of us to enter. I thought about the story I'd written at Aldama Elementary. What if my writing was rejected again? But now I spoke English well enough and I hoped I might have a chance this time. What if by some miracle I did win? Would Papi finally be proud of me?

So far, making my father proud had been impossible. He'd never once come to my band concerts. He didn't go to Carlos's soccer games. He didn't go to Mago's performances with her modern dance class at Franklin High School. So how could I ever hope to make my father finally take notice? I didn't know. I just knew I needed to try.

Due to the influence of Sweet Valley High, I wrote a short story about identical twins—Beverly and Kimberly. But in my story the twins were separated when their parents divorced. The mother kept Beverly, and the father took Kimberly far away. One day when they were teenagers, the twins were reunited, and now they were strangers to each other. They had to struggle to feel like sisters again. It was a sad story, but that was the world I lived in, the world I knew. Wasn't that exactly what had happened between me and Betty?

I turned in my short story, and for the following two

weeks I was anxious about the results. What if my story got rejected? Would I find the strength to keep writing, or would I give it up for good?

When the time came to find out the results, they were given through the PA system during homeroom. "Congratulations to all the students who entered the short-story contest," the principal said over the speaker. I held my breath and put my head between my hands. "Remember, even if you didn't place, you're still a winner."

She started off with the honorable mentions, but my name wasn't one of them. Then she announced the third-place winner. It wasn't me. Then the second-place winner. It wasn't me, and by now tears were starting to form. "And the first-place winner is—Reyna Grande."

I looked at the speaker. Had I just heard my name? My homeroom teacher clapped and said, "Congratulations, Reyna. I'm so proud of you." All the students looked at me, and for the first time they weren't looking at me to criticize me but to congratulate me.

When I went to English class, my teacher had the competition prize for me. In front of the whole class, she handed me my prize and a blue ribbon that read *First Place*. There were two tickets stapled to a brochure. On the front of the brochure was a picture of a beautiful cruise ship.

Had I just won two tickets to go on a cruise? My heart started to race. Wouldn't Papi finally be proud of me when he found out that I was taking him on a cruise!

"These are tickets to go to the *Queen Mary*," my teacher said.

"The *Queen Mary*?" I asked. I glanced at the picture of the cruise ship. What a beautiful name for a ship. But I'd never heard of it before. "Where is it?"

"In Long Beach," she said.

I didn't know where Long Beach was either, but I was so excited just thinking about the adventure I was going to have on that cruise and how much fun it would be to share it with Papi. Maybe we could have a father-daughter moment when we could finally bond, where we could finally feel like a real family. I imagined us standing on the deck as the ship pulled away from the harbor. I pictured us holding hands, hands that were the exact same shape, and not letting go as we became surrounded in azure.

"You do know what the *Queen Mary* is, right?" my teacher asked, interrupting my thoughts.

When I shook my head, she told me a brief history about the cruise ship, except I stopped listening when she got to the part where she told me the *Queen Mary* didn't go anywhere! Why in the world would the school give me tickets for a cruise ship that didn't go on cruises?

I went back to my seat, and for the rest of the day I couldn't stop thinking about the adventure I had thought I was going to share with my father.

Despite the disappointment about the cruise, I went home feeling proud. I couldn't wait for Papi to come home so I could give him the news. As soon as he opened the door, I ran to him. "I got first place in a competition!" I showed him the prize and my short story.

Papi glanced at the tickets. "What in the world is the Queen Mary?" he said.

"It's a cruise ship, except . . . it doesn't go anywhere."

"So what's the point of going to see it?" he said.

"Because I won!" I said.

"I don't even know where it is."

"It's in Long Beach."

"Long Beach is a big place," he said. "I don't want to get lost."

"Couldn't we ask for directions?" I asked. But I already knew what his final answer was. Like most immigrants, Papi didn't go anywhere unless he knew where he was going. He didn't want to risk being pulled over by the police and end up deported.

Without another word Papi handed me back my prize and short story. I put my prize and ribbon inside a little box where I stored my keepsakes. I told myself the prize wasn't important. What mattered was that my writing hadn't been rejected! I took out my notebook and found a clean page. Then I started to write another story.

15

"See that boy there, the one with green eyes?" my friend Phuong said to me one day as she pointed to the other side of the cafeteria. When I spotted the boy she was pointing to, I nodded. Phuong said, "I love him. Go talk him for me." She pushed me toward him, but I didn't move. How could I go up to a complete stranger to talk to him about my friend? She said his name was Luis and he was from El Salvador. He had just started ESL class and didn't speak much English. Phuong didn't speak much English either, and that was why she hadn't passed to regular classes like I had.

Phuong wanted me to act as her messenger, and she told me what to tell Luis in Spanish for her. She said, "Reyna, you and me are sisters. You need help me." Phuong said we were like sisters because I look Asian, just like her.

I finally gathered up the nerve to go talk to Luis during nutrition class the following day, and I told him my friend Phuong loved him, just like she'd told me to tell him. Luis laughed and said, "She hardly knows me, so how can she love me?"

I didn't know what to say to him then, because as he looked at me with those green eyes of his, I knew that I—just like Phuong—was a goner. His eyes were velvety green, like the mountains that surround Iguala. I found myself looking at him, and I felt like I was home. The ache I had in my heart whenever I thought about Iguala was gone. He was wrong. It was possible to love someone even if you hardly knew them.

Every day I delivered messages to him from Phuong, but that only took a minute or two, and after that he asked me questions, but not about Phuong, about me.

"Where do you live?"

"On Granada and Avenue 50," I said.

"Really? I live there too!"

It turned out he lived on the south side of Granada!

Phuong wasn't stupid. She wasn't able to speak Spanish and couldn't really understand what we were saying to each other from where she waited, but by the end of the week, Phuong wasn't talking to me anymore. She said, "You bad sister, Reyna Grande," and then turned and walked away.

I guess I wasn't meant to be anyone's cupid.

One day I was heading down Avenue 50, and from the corner of my eye I saw Luis riding his bike on the opposite side. He didn't pedal but let gravity pull him down the street. In this way he kept pace with me as I made my way to the liquor store to buy Papi a bottle of charcoal lighter fluid. As I went into the store, I turned to look at Luis. He waited there at the corner on his bike.

I came out of Barney's Liquors, and I knew I should hurry home because Papi was making carne asada on the grill and was waiting for me to come back. But Luis waved at me from across the street and motioned for me to come over. The light wasn't even green yet, but my feet were already pointed in his direction, and I took a step onto the street. The light had turned green by the time I was halfway to Luis and his emerald eyes.

He said, "Let's go for a walk," and he got off his bike and walked alongside me. He didn't talk much, and I didn't either. Ours was a silent love. I glanced at him from the corner of my eye. He had curly hair, curlier than mine, and it was the color of crushed brown sugar. Luis said, "Have you ever been kissed?" and I shook my head, feeling the ground turn into mud beneath my feet. I felt a rushing in my head, and I looked into his green eyes. I thought of the vacant lot by Abuela Evila's house, of Carlos, Mago, and me driving the old car toward the Mountain That Has a Headache. Except now it was the mountain that was moving toward me, and I got lost in its velvety beauty.

Papi said, "Where have you been?"

I glanced off into the distance, and in my dreamy haze I handed over the lighter fluid and walked past Papi and

241

the grill. I wondered if Luis was thinking about me and about the kiss we'd just shared. My lips were still throbbing.

Papi whacked me on the head with his hand. "Answer me," he said.

"They didn't have any lighter fluid at the liquor store, so I had to go to the store on Avenue 52," I said.

He said, "I'm not stupid, girl. I know you're lying. As long as you live under my roof, you aren't going to lie to me. Now, where were you?"

I couldn't tell him about my first kiss. He'd beat me for sure, ruin the whole memory of it. And why couldn't he just let me be so I could run to my room and think about Luis and our first kiss?

"Answer me now!" he said, putting a hand on his belt.

"I don't have to live under your roof if I don't want to," I said defiantly. "Whenever I want, I can go live with my mother."

I turned around and headed out the door. I walked toward the corner of Avenue 50 as if I were on my way to catch the bus. I didn't really mean to leave, but I was tired of Papi always making me feel as if *he* were our only option. Maybe he was. Mami had never once asked us to live with her. How would we have fit into that tiny room of hers? But Papi didn't need to know that. All he needed to know was that I wouldn't let him treat me like a child anymore, because I had now officially been kissed—even before Mago.

Luis and his friends were sitting on the cinder-block wall of the house on the corner. He and his friends whistled at me. Luis shouted something, and I didn't hear what he said, but the next thing I knew, my hair felt as if it had caught on something and was tearing out of my scalp.

"You're not going anywhere!" Papi said from behind me. He pulled me back to the house by my hair, and I yelled for him to let me go. Luis and his friends whistled louder, and I thought I heard them laughing. I couldn't see Luis through my tears, but I knew he was there, witnessing my shame. Papi took me into the house, and Mago and Carlos begged him to let me go, but he took off his belt and whipped me with it. I thought about Luis and his green eyes, and soon I didn't even feel the sting of the belt.

On Monday during nutrition I went in search of Luis. I wondered if he was going to ask me to be his girlfriend, now that we'd shared a kiss. But when I came up to him and his friends, Luis glanced at me and then turned around as if I weren't there. His friends pointed at me, and Luis shook his head and didn't turn to look at me. Farther down the cafeteria I saw Phuong with her Asian friends. She smirked and then turned away from me, and it hurt me to know I'd lost my friend for a boy who was no longer interested in me. Was I a bad kisser? Was that why he didn't want to talk to me? Or was it that Papi had humiliated me in front of him and now he thought

243

I was still a little girl because I'd gotten beaten by my father? I touched the right side of my thigh where Papi's belt buckle had left a raised tattoo. Maybe Luis thought like my father and like my mother. Maybe it was just too easy to leave me.

I headed to my favorite spot—the steps that led up to the band room. Mr. Adams wasn't there now, so I sat on the steps and took out my V. C. Andrews book, because she, at least, was still my friend.

16

Five years after we arrived in the U.S., Mago made history. She became the first person in our family—from both sides—to get a high school diploma. I became the third person (after Mago and Carlos) to graduate from junior high. My little accomplishment might not have been much to be proud of, but I told myself that was just the beginning. Through all of his talks of the future, my father had taught me to dream big dreams.

When my father beat me and insulted me when he was drunk, I'd hold on to the dreams he had given me. I would think about those dreams when the blows came, because the father who beat me, the one who preferred to stay home and drink rather than attend my band concerts or parent-teacher conferences, wasn't the same father who would tell me that one day I'd be somebody in this country. That much I knew.

A second thing to celebrate was that finally, the month before, we had become legal residents of the United States! It was just in time for Mago to not worry about being able to attend college. In Mexico the biggest dream Mago had had was to be a lawyer's secretary. Now Mago didn't want to be a secretary—she wanted to be the lawyer who had a secretary. This was what Papi had taught us—that here in this country we could be anything!

Papi took out a five-thousand-dollar loan under his name to help her with her college expenses because he said his "Negra" was going to make us proud. When she started college in the fall, I would start high school.

In the summer I went to marching band camp at Franklin High School. I explored the campus while it was empty. It was twice as big as Burbank! My schools just kept getting bigger and bigger. I wondered what a college campus looked like. I wondered if Mago would feel lost. I wished I was old enough to go to college with her so that we could help each other find our way.

The summer went by quickly, and soon September was here. I would finally turn fifteen! I wouldn't be having a Quinceañera, as I had always dreamed of. Papi said those parties were too expensive. A few months ago we had finally moved into the three-bedroom apartment so Mago, Carlos, and I could have privacy. Papi had finally realized we were too old to be sleeping in the living room! Now with their part of the mortgage being much more than before, Papi said there was no money for anything, especially a party.

"I'll take you to Raging Waters, Chata," he said. The

week before, he'd told us we would go to the water park on Labor Day weekend. It'd be my first time ever, and I was excited about it, but he couldn't fool me.

"We aren't going there to celebrate my fifteenth birthday," I said. "We're going because Kingsley Manor is having an employee picnic."

"I wouldn't go if it wasn't for your birthday," he said.

I replied to him in English, with a word I'd picked up at school from other kids. "Whatever."

A few days before our trip to Raging Waters, I came home exhausted after band practice. Mago arrived soon after. Together we cleaned the house and made sure all our chores were done before Papi got home. He didn't like coming home to a dirty house. Carlos wasn't back yet. This whole summer he'd been going to the park to play soccer with his friends. We'd told him to get back before Papi arrived from work. Papi didn't like to have us out in the streets, but he'd given Carlos permisison as long as he didn't get back too late.

But soon Papi and Mila came home and there was still no sign of Carlos. "Where is your brother?" Papi asked.

"We don't know."

He grabbed a beer from the fridge and went to his room while we helped Mila with dinner.

It was seven o'clock and we still had no idea what was keeping Carlos. He'd never stayed out this late at the

247

park. "Should we go look for him?" we asked.

Papi shook his head. "You can't be walking around at night by yourselves. Besides, your brother is already in big trouble, with me."

Mago and I went into our room. While I practiced my sax, Mago bleached her arm hair. Now that she had a part-time job at a collections agency, she was always doing things to herself. She'd bought tons of makeup and was always practicing in front of the mirror, but no matter how much she put on, she couldn't hide the scars on her face to her satisfaction.

"Come here, Nena. I'll do your arms. They're hairier than mine," she said. "And look, when you bleach the hair, it makes your skin look lighter!" She extended her arm out for me to see.

What saved me from getting my arm hair bleached was the front door being opened. We ran out to the living room to see two men carrying Carlos in.

"What happened?" Mago said as we rushed to help. Carlos's face was pale and covered in sweat. He groaned with every step the men took as they carried him over to the couch.

"His leg is hurt," one of the men said as he wiped his dirty, sweaty face with his soccer shirt.

"One of the guys from the other team tried to get the ball from him and kicked his shin instead of the ball," the other guy said. "Your brother doesn't have shin guards. I think the leg is broken."

We thanked the men, and they left. Carlos was trying hard to keep from crying. I knew he was trying to be strong so that we wouldn't see him cry.

"I told you!" Papi yelled as he came out of his room. "I told you to stop going to the park. I told you to stay out of trouble, but you don't listen to me!"

He turned around to go back to his room.

"Where are you going?" Mago said. "You have to take him to the hospital!"

"Well, I'm not going to," Papi said. "That will teach him a lesson." Then he went to his room and slammed his door shut.

Mago and I looked at each other in horror. *How can he not take him to the hospital? What if his leg really is broken?* We turned to look at Mila, who was standing by the kitchen. We waited for her to say that *she* would take our brother. Hadn't it always been she who had taken us to the doctor, anyway? Instead she said, "Let me try to convince him," and went into their bedroom.

We sat on the couch with Carlos. He winced in pain at any little movement. He said, "It really hurts, Mago. I can't stand it anymore." And he finally broke into tears. I couldn't remember the last time I'd seen him cry. Even when Papi beat him, he'd hold in his tears and wouldn't cry, even if it made Papi get madder and hit him harder.

Mago got up and went to knock on Papi's bedroom door. I didn't know why Mila hadn't come back out. "You can't leave him like that! He's in a lot of pain!" Mago said

249

as she banged on the door. But there was no answer.

Mago went to the kitchen to boil water. She came back with a pot of hot water, a salt container, and clean kitchen towels. She poured the salt into the hot water and said maybe it'd keep the swelling down.

I wished I had the courage to do something. Call 911. Go get the neighbors. Something. Mago and I glanced at each other and quickly looked away, shame choking us up inside, for neither of us were courageous enough to defy our father.

All night long we took turns putting hot towels on Carlos's leg. We gave him aspirin and tried to get him to sleep. It was a long night for the three of us. I thought about those nights in Mexico, of how Mago had helped us pass the time by telling us stories about our father, by digging out the memories that made her happy. But tonight, as Carlos and I looked at her for comfort, she couldn't say anything.

What was there to say?

I thought about the Man Behind the Glass. I wished I hadn't left him behind. In his eternal silence he had been a much better father than the one we lived with now.

Morning came, and Papi still refused to take Carlos to the hospital. "I'm not going to miss work because of your brother's stupidity," he told us. We looked at Mila, pleading with her, but she simply looked away, not wanting to go against Papi's wishes. They both left for work.

250

With a heavy heart Mago left for work too. "I'm going to come back with help. I promise," she said.

Today was my last day of summer band practice, and Carlos said I shouldn't miss it. He said, "Go. I'll be fine."

"I can't leave you like this," I said.

At work Mago told her coworkers about our dilemma, and many of them volunteered to take Carlos to the hospital. They arrived during their lunch hour. It took five people to get Carlos out of the house, two supporting him by his shoulders, and the other three holding up his legs, being especially careful with the left leg to keep it from moving. Any little movement made Carlos cry out in pain.

Just as they were about to put him into the car, Papi got home. "I came to take him to the hospital," he said as he got out of his truck.

"Well, it's too late now," Mago said. "*I'm* the one who is taking him."

"He's my son. I'll take him."

Mago stared angrily at Papi, and I thought she was going to argue with him about it. But she was smart enough to realize that Carlos had to get to the hospital, and it didn't matter who took him, as long as someone did. She asked her coworkers to put Carlos inside Papi's truck. They ended up putting him in the bed of the truck so Carlos could keep his leg straight. We watched as Papi drove away, and my poor brother winced every time the truck went over a pothole.

He came home with his leg in a cast. Both the tibia and fibula had broken.

"That's the only way your father knows how to be," Mila said to us later that evening. "He was abused by his parents, so that's all he knows."

We didn't tell Mila we were sick and tired of her justifying Papi's behavior with the same lame excuses. We understood what Papi must have gone through, because we knew firsthand what our grandparents were like. But that didn't make us feel better. If Papi knew how it felt to be abused by his parents, then shouldn't he understand how *we* felt? Shouldn't he try to be a better father?

"I came back for you, didn't I?" he would say to us sometimes when we spoke up.

Then we'd shut up and lower our heads, and we'd continue to take his beatings. Even the day when he punched me in the nose so hard that it broke, even as I looked at the drops of blood landing on my white tennis shoe one by one, I told myself maybe he was right. We shouldn't expect anything better from him. He didn't forget us, after all. We were here because of him. *I* was in this country because of him. I had *begged* him to bring me. I'd gotten what I wanted, after all. How could I complain now, simply because things weren't what we'd once hoped for?

On Labor Day weekend we went to Raging Waters as planned. Mago brought her boyfriend, Juan, a guy she'd met at school—her first "official" boyfriend since Papi had finally given her permission to date. They told me I could

252

hang out with them, but I knew I was just going to be in the way. Besides, I didn't like Juan. Not that there was anything wrong with him. It was just that now, instead of spending time with me, Mago spent her free time with him. I wished Papi hadn't allowed her to have a boyfriend. But Mago was turning nineteen the following month, and even Papi couldn't keep her from growing up. I was afraid of the day when she'd no longer be my Mago but someone else's.

Mila and Papi spent the day together too, talking to their coworkers. Because Carlos's leg was in a cast, he had no choice but to stay in the same spot, watching over our stuff. I spent the day by myself. I walked from one side of the park to the other, wondering what rides to go on. Most of the kids had someone to ride with. I seemed to be the only person in Raging Waters who was alone.

After a few rides on my own, I decided to call it quits and went back to hang out with Carlos. "Why don't you go on the rides?" he asked, looking longingly at the blue pools glittering in the sun and the big waterslides all around us. So many years dreaming about swimming in the pools of La Quinta Castrejón, and now that we were in a place a hundred times more beautiful, we couldn't enjoy it.

"It sucks going on them alone," I said.

"Well, it sure sucks being here like this," he said, raising one of his crutches. So he and I sat there, watching kids run around, dripping wet, going from ride to ride, laughing and screaming, until finally it was time to go home.

253

17

After Carlos broke his leg, things weren't the same between Mago and Papi. It wasn't something one could see right away, but I knew my sister better than I knew myself. Before, she used to take pride in coming home on paydays and would happily hand over half of her salary to Papi to help him with the household expenses. Now he practically had to pull the money out of her hand. Her fingers hesitated for a second too long before they released the bills. Papi didn't notice it. He didn't know her the way I did.

She no longer had the feverish desire to be the best in school to make Papi happy. Even though she was now the first person in our family to attend college, she was no longer concerned about being the "best and brightest" in her classes. Instead she talked about looking for a full-time job and buying herself a car and pretty clothes. She wanted to go out with her coworkers, who spent their weekends dancing at clubs.

"Papi doesn't want for you to be out partying," I told her.

She shrugged and said, "I don't care what he likes or doesn't like."

And just like that, the father she'd longed for in Mexico, the father she'd dreamed would be her hero, vanished in her eyes. Unfortunately, it wasn't the same for me. I couldn't stop wanting to please him. I couldn't let go of my desire to hear him tell me he didn't regret bringing me to the U.S.

One day in November, I was walking with Mago on Figueroa Street after she'd made a payment at Fashion 21 for the clothes she'd put on layaway. We passed by the shops and looked longingly at the shoes and pretty clothes the mannequins in the windows were wearing. As we passed by a dress boutique, Mago stopped abruptly and pulled me with her to the display window. A mannequin was wearing the most beautiful Quinceañera dress we'd ever seen. We stood there in silence admiring it.

I looked at Mago, wondering if she felt bad about not having had a real Quinceañera. When she'd turned sixteen, Papi had thrown her a party, though not a real Quinceañera. The party had been held in the six-car parking lot at the apartments. Mago had worn the long, puffy, blue dress she'd worn at her junior high graduation and had had her hair permed into tight curls.

Now, as she looked longingly at the dress the mannequin wore, I wanted to remind her of that party, tell her that a sixteenth-birthday party in a parking lot was better than no party at all, but I didn't. I thought about those nights in Iguala when we'd sold goodies with our mother at La Quinta Castrejón and watched all those young girls with their beautiful Quinceañera dresses. I recognized that look of longing in her eyes, and I knew that if I could have seen myself in a mirror at that moment, I would have seen that same look in my own eyes.

"You know what, Nena? I'm going to throw you a Quinceañera."

"What are you talking about? You're crazy," I said. "I already turned fifteen two months ago. And besides, where are you going to get the money?"

"I don't know, but I'll get it. I'll ask my friends to be the godparents. But I'll do it."

I thought my sister was nuts. Quinceañeras were expensive, and there was no way Mago, with her part-time job, could pull it off.

When we got home, Mago got on the phone with her friends and shared her plan. She didn't want to tell Papi about it. "This is *my* gift to you," she said. "I don't want him to have anything to do with this." But I insisted that she tell him. Who knew? He might actually get excited about it. This might be a way for them to repair their relationship.

I finally managed to convince her, but when she told Papi about it, he was even more skeptical than me. "You're crazy," he said, and didn't offer to help.

I tried not to get excited about the Quinceañera,

knowing that pretty soon Mago would come to her senses and realize it wasn't going to happen. To my surprise, on Sunday when we visited Mami, she got on board with the Quinceañera and offered to find some godparents to help with the expenses.

"I can't believe Mami wants to help," I told Mago later.

"I'm not," she said, "Don't you remember those nights at La Quinta Castrejón?" And I suddenly knew what she meant. Those nights at La Quinta, we weren't the only ones watching girls blooming out of limousines like pink peonies. Mami was too. Mami, who also had never had a Quinceañera, who had also once been a starry-eyed girl with glittery dreams.

Not even a week had gone by when Mami called to say a friend of hers would be the godparent for the cake, another would take care of the catering, and she herself would pay for the DJ. Mago's friends offered to help pay for the hall, the mass, the photographer, the floral arrangements, the souvenirs. Mago didn't look for a godparent for the dress. She was buying me my Quinceañera dress herself. She set the date for May 2, which left us a little over five months.

Mago's excitement was contagious. Even Carlos wanted to participate. He offered to be one of my escorts and helped me find a chambelán, the boy who would be my escort and dance partner during the waltz. I also asked my girlfriends to be my ladies-in-waiting, and luckily, their families gave them permission.

Mago hired a professional dressmaker to make me a real Cinderella dress! The bottom part was made of layers and layers of blue tulle. The bodice was made of white satin, and the sleeves were decorated with blue satin bows. I looked like a princess, just as I'd always dreamed I would.

The day finally arrived, and I found myself standing outside the church at Placita Olvera about to have a mass in my honor. I was officially going to become a little woman in the eyes of God. The problem was that in order to have this mass, we'd had to lie to the priest about me having done my first communion. That was a requirement for the mass. Mago had told the priest I'd done my first communion in Mexico but didn't have the certificate to prove it. He believed us, and I felt terrible afterward for lying to the priest.

The organ player started to play, and my court, composed of six couples, began to walk into the church in pairs. I held on to my escort, who was a friend of my brother's. He was a sweet boy, but there was nothing romantic between us. This was strictly business. He was there to hold my hand, take pictures with me, and dance the waltz with me, but the next day he would go on with his life and I with mine. I thought about Axel, the clarinet player at Franklin I had a crush on. His family had not allowed him to participate in my Quinceañera as my escort. I wished he were here with me instead of this boy I hardly knew.

My heart started to beat faster as I came into the church.

258

Right away my eyes fell onto the statue of Jesus Christ hanging on the wall. *Forgive me for my lie, Jesus.* I held on to my chambelán as we walked down the aisle. People smiled at me and congratulated me. Papi and Mila were sitting to my left. Mago, Mami, Betty, Rey, and my little brother, Leonardo, were sitting to my right.

Too soon we got to the altar, and I knelt before the priest. Jesus looked down on me from his cross, and my eyes started to burn because I was about to commit a grave sin—to take Holy Communion when I wasn't supposed to. I turned to look at Mago, who was sitting in the front pew. I wanted her to stop this. I wanted her to tell the priest we had lied and I shouldn't be having this mass. But she was so excited, my sister, so proud of what she had accomplished today, I knew I must go through with this no matter what. I couldn't ruin the party my sister had worked so hard to give me.

The dreaded moment came when Holy Communion began and the priest said, "The body of Christ," and put the host onto my tongue.

"Amen," I replied.

The wafer got stuck to the roof of my mouth as soon as I closed it. Tears filled my eyes as the host began to dissolve, and I pictured Jesus bursting down from heaven in a blinding beam of light and sending me straight to the worst hell imaginable, a hell where I would spend all of eternity alone, without my Mago. Even though I wanted to stop being overshadowed by my sister and her

259

bigger-than-life personality, I was terrified of being without her, of being on my own. Of making my way in the world without her by my side. *Forgive me, Jesus. Please, don't take my sister away from me.*

After mass we took pictures outside the church. "Nena, smile!" Mago said as the photographer took picture after picture. But I couldn't do it, and in all the pictures I looked as if I were attending a funeral.

As we headed to Los Feliz to take pictures at Mulholland Fountain on the corner of Riverside Drive and Los Feliz Boulevard, I told Mago what was on my mind. "I'm going to go to hell. I've committed a grave sin." I started to cry. She started to laugh.

"Nena, all that is nonsense. First of all, there is no hell or the devil. Those are just stories Abuela Evila liked to frighten us with. Come on, when are you going to stop believing in that? Use that imagination of yours for other things. Second of all, if there *is* a hell, we're already living in it." She wiped away my tears and hugged me. From then on I smiled in the pictures, and I didn't think about my fear of being punished for lying to the priest.

The reception was held at the Masonic Temple on Figueroa Street. That night was a night when my wishes came true. I'd wished to have my father and mother together in the same room. Now here they were, although on opposite sides of the banquet hall. My mother was running around helping serve food to the guests. She was wearing a black dress covered in sequins. She'd even had her hair done at a beauty salon. I'd never seen her looking so glamorous. My father was on the opposite side of the room wearing a long-sleeve shirt and tie, sitting next to Mila. She took sips of her soda while my father drank beer after beer. The photographer called them over and took pictures of us. First I took one with my mother. Then I took one with my father. And just as he was walking away, I pulled his arm back and I took one with both, my father and mother on either side of me.

Finally it was time for the part of the waltz where I got to dance with my father, but I didn't feel those over-powering emotions I thought I'd feel when I finally danced with him. My heart wasn't racing, my palms weren't sweating, my head wasn't spinning. I didn't feel a thing. I smelled the alcohol on his breath and I kept turning my face away from his. Always my eyes returned to my sister standing by the door looking proudly at me. And I knew I should have been dancing the waltz with her.

18

Ever since she'd gotten her green card, Mami would go to Mexico every year. She'd pull Leonardo and Betty out of Ninth Street Elementary and take them with her. Rey stayed in LA to tend their booth at the swap meet, where they now sold cosmetics.

Mago, Carlos, and I had yet to visit Iguala. When Tía Emperatriz stole my father's house, he said he would not return to the place of his birth. "What for?" he said. "I have nothing there." So he'd never taken us back for a visit.

But one day Mago surprised me when she announced she wanted to go to Mexico with Mami. I thought it was because she missed our family and the place we'd once called home. I knew I did. Instead, Mago was going because her best friend, Gaby, wanted to go to Acapulco, a three-hour bus ride from Iguala. "I'll go with you to Iguala for a few days only," Mago told Mami when we picked her up to go to the travel agency. "Then I'll join my friend."

Mago had recently bought herself a brand-new Toyota

Tercel. The car smelled of new plastic and coconut. I felt sad to know what this car had cost my sister. A brand-new car comes with a big monthly bill. Not long after buying herself this car, Mago had to find a full-time job selling ads for a newspaper. She had too much debt from the clothes and pretty shoes she bought herself. It was as if she were trying to make up for all those years in Mexico when we only had rags to wear. I'd go with her to May Co., Robinson's, and the Broadway to make payments on her credit cards, but she was never able to pay them down. She'd say, "I'm sick of the old ladies' clothes Mila brings us from work! I want to dress my own way, develop my own style." She flicked her hair, which was now dyed a dark brown with golden highlights, and said, "Never again will I wear hand-me-downs!"

If any of her friends in Mexico had looked at her now, they wouldn't recognize her. Sometimes I hardly recognized her myself. My sister was becoming a classy young woman for sure. But between the credit card debt and the car loan, Mago had dropped out of college to work full time.

As we were sitting with the travel agent, Mago surprised me. "Do you want to go, Nena?"

"Wait. What? But I don't have any money," I said.

"When do you ever?" she said, rolling her eyes. "I'm offering to buy you the plane ticket. Do you want to go or not?"

I touched my belly button, something I hadn't done in a long time. The yearning for my native country was still there, although it shamed me to realize that the yearning

263

wasn't as strong as it had been. I thought about all those credit card bills Mago had, her car payment, the bill for the telephone line she'd installed in our bedroom, the money she had to give our father for household expenses. I thought about the student loans she still had to repay for a college education she'd given up on.

"I don't know," I said. As much as I wanted to go, I also didn't want her to spend any more money. I'd rather she used it to return to school.

"I know you want to go," she said. She handed over her credit card to the travel agent and purchased our tickets.

Mago, Mami, Leonardo, Betty, and I went to Mexico a few weeks later. Carlos couldn't come because of his responsibilities now that he was head of his own household. Just like Mago, he'd dropped out of college after less than a year to marry his high school girlfriend. Now he had two jobs and no time for school.

"Reyna can't go with you," Papi said to Mago when we got home. "Are you crazy? Your sister will miss a whole week of school!"

"Well, you're going to have to let her go. The tickets are nonrefundable, and they were expensive," she said.

I felt awful about having to miss school. I could count on one hand the times I'd missed: in fifth grade when I'd had lice, seventh grade when I'd had the chicken pox, eighth grade when we'd had to go to Tijuana to the

American embassy to process our paperwork for our legal residency. And now my senior year.

"Please, Papi. Can I go? I miss Mexico. I miss my grandmother."

"I said no," Papi said. "First your sister drops out of college. Then your brother drops out. And now you want to miss an entire week of school? Haven't I taught you anything? You kids are so ungrateful. Coming to this country was an opportunity of a lifetime, and you're just wasting it away. People would kill to have a green card, and look at you, not appreciating its worth."

I felt ashamed, but I still refused to give up on the trip. In the end Papi gave in when I came home with the assignments my teachers had given me so I wouldn't fall behind while I was gone. As much as I hated missing school and not getting that perfect attendance certificate I loved to get at the end of a semester, I was desperate to return to the country of my birth.

I didn't know what to expect on my return to Mexico. I'd been in the United States for eight years. I was seventeen years old, and the poor little girl who'd been born in a shack was gone. I had changed, though not as much as Mago.

As we made our way to Abuelita Chinta's house, we drove across the bridge over the river where my cousin Catalina had drowned. Except now it wasn't as much a river as a dumping place for trash.

265

"That's disgusting!" Mago said as we got hit with the smell of rotten water.

We passed by the train station, and I was shocked to see it completely empty. "Where are the vendors? Where are the travelers?" I asked the taxi driver.

He told us that a year before, the government had sold the railroad system, and the train in Iguala had been suspended. There were no more passengers coming through there every day. There were no more vendors, no more food stands with the delicious scent of chicken quesadillas, no more people from local towns coming to catch the train. Men, like my uncles, who'd depended on the freight trains to make a living had found it even harder to survive.

As we sped down the road, I looked at the empty train station, feeling my eyes burn with tears, thinking about what Iguala had lost.

Since we had too many suitcases, the taxi driver had to take us all the way to my grandmother's, instead of dropping us off at the main road. He drove over the unpaved road full of holes and jutting rocks.

"Jeez," Mago said as she held on for dear life as we got tossed around in the car. "I can't believe these roads. They would ruin my car for sure!"

My heart started to beat faster when we pulled up in front of my grandmother's little shack. I knew I'd been in the U.S. for too long when the sight of the shack—with its bamboo sticks, corrugated metal roof, and tar-soaked cardboard—shocked me. Did I really live in this place?

A few feet away from the house was an abandoned freight car left to rust on the tracks. Five kids were playing in it. At seeing those kids' dusty bare feet, dirty hair, and torn clothing, I knew how my father had seen us those many years before when he'd returned. I wondered if his heart had broken at seeing us like that.

Tía Güera and Abuelita Chinta came out to greet us. My aunt lived in a shack next to my grandmother's. She'd returned to Mexico a few years before because she hadn't liked the United States. She held a baby girl in her arms. Then she turned to the kids playing in the abandoned freight car and called out the names Lupita and Angel. A boy and a girl got up and came running.

"Say hello to your cousins and your aunt," Tía Güera told them.

My grandmother's face was mapped with more wrinkles, her hair was mostly gray now, and a few more teeth had fallen out. But when she hugged me, I breathed in her scent of almond oil and herbs, and I couldn't believe I was back in my grandmother's arms. Her scent was all I needed to know I was home.

"I have prayed for this moment for so long," Abuelita Chinta said, squeezing me tight. "God has finally answered my prayers."

I was five feet, zero inches. I was so used to looking up at everyone, it felt weird to look down at my tiny grandmother. She was three inches shorter than me!

How tiny and fragile she seemed to me now.

We went into the shack with her, and not long after we'd sat down to eat the meal Abuelita Chinta had made for us, Mago began to complain again. "Look at my shoes," she said. "They're covered in dust. Ugh."

"Get over it," I said, thinking about my grandmother's feet. Hadn't Mago seen the layer of dust on her feet, the dirt caked under her toenails? Abuelita Chinta gave Mago a rag to wipe her shoes and feet with.

After our meal Tío Gary arrived with his children in tow. I was shocked to see how skinny my uncle was. A rope was tied around his waist to hold up his pants. He had four boys. The youngest had leukemia, and my uncle said he had no money for treatment.

"Why don't you go to El Otro Lado, Gary?" my mother asked my uncle. "You can give your children a better life if you do. You can afford a doctor."

My uncle shook his head. "I'd rather be poor but together," he said.

I thought about my own father, and the choice he'd made to go north, the price we'd paid for that decision. Was my uncle right? Was it better to be poor but together? Or was it better to try to find a better life, even if it meant breaking up your family?

If Papi hadn't made the choice to leave, and later taken us with him, I would still have been there in Mexico, in that poverty. Not in high school, not on my way to college as I was now. Papi was right. My siblings and I had been given the opportunity of a lifetime. How could we let it go to waste? As I looked at my cousins dressed in rags, barefoot, and with bellies full of tapeworm, I thought of my father, of what he wanted for our future, and I understood.

I took advantage of being there and quickly set out to look for the friends I'd left behind. Some of them were already married and had children! Others were still living at home and working as maids, or at the U.S.-owned factory nearby, or whatever else they could find. But things had changed. When you come from the U.S., people look at you differently. They treat you differently.

The boys looked at me as if they wanted to marry me on the spot so that I could take them back with me to El Otro Lado. My girlfriends didn't invite me into their houses like they used to. Now they stood outside with me and blocked the entrance to their houses with their bodies, and I knew it was because they were embarrassed. I wasn't offered anything to eat or drink, because they couldn't afford to feed themselves, let alone a guest. They didn't tell me much about their lives because it could never compare to *my* life, now that I was living in that beautiful place they all yearned for.

Instead I awkwardly stood with my seventeen-year-old friend Meche in front of her shack. I didn't know what to say to her as she held her baby in her arms and tried to wipe the dirt and mucus off his face with the corner of her blouse. She didn't look at me. She looked past me, at the huizache trees behind me.

I was determined to make her see I was still the same Reyna, but I didn't know how to do it. In the U.S. the only people I spoke Spanish with were my mother and father. With everyone else I spoke in English. And as I stood there trying to talk with Meche, I kept stumbling on my Spanish words. She laughed and said I spoke like a pocha, a Mexican born in the U.S. I felt ashamed to realize that learning English had cost me my Spanish.

It was an awkward conversation. I tried to think of something else to talk about besides school, marching band, my writing, books, and the colleges I'd applied to. I was afraid to admit that I might not be the same little girl who used to make tortillas out of mud and whose only dream of the future was to one day have her parents back.

As I walked away from Meche's house, I realized there was something I'd lost the day I'd left my hometown. Even though my umbilical cord was buried in Iguala, I was no longer considered Mexican enough. To the people there, who'd seen me grow up, I was no longer one of them.

"Where have you been?" Mago asked the minute I got back. "I'm the one who brought you here, remember? You can't just do what you want. I wanted to leave for Acapulco today. I'm so sick of this place. Now look what time it is."

"I wanted to spend time with my friends before we leave," I said.

270

She pointed to the shacks on the other side of the canal where Meche lived and said, "I don't know why you want to be over there with that trash."

"What do you mean 'trash'?" I asked. "Have you forgotten this is where you come from?" I was so furious, and before I could stop myself, I pushed her.

"Just because I used to live here, it doesn't mean that I still need to be friends with those people," she said, and pushed me back. "Let them dare call me a little orphan now."

"You conceited brat," I said, pushing her even harder.

The next thing I knew, Mago and I were pulling each other's hair and tumbling down to the ground.

"Reyna, Reyna, leave your sister alone!" Mami yelled. But I couldn't stop. I didn't know why I was so angry at my sister. How could she just cut the ties that bound us to this place? To these friends of ours who weren't able to escape this poverty like we had? I was so angry at her for quitting college and hurting her chances for a successful life. Now I realized we owed it to them, our cousins, our friends, to do something with our lives. If not for us, then for them, because they'd never be able to. I understood clearly now why Papi had said there were so many people who would die to have the opportunities we had, who would kill to get their hands on a green card, which we were lucky enough to have gotten. Mago's refusal to see that angered me more than anything else.

"Stop! Stop!" Mami said. And finally I did. Mago looked at me as if she didn't know me. I ran into my grandmother's house crying and feeling ashamed. For the first time in my life, I had raised a hand to my sister.

How could I stop myself from feeling sad that Mago no longer cared about Iguala? Sad that she didn't think of this place as special because it had once been our home? Her home was now the U.S. Unlike me, she had no accent when she spoke English. Now I knew why that was. Even in her speech she was trying to erase Mexico completely.

I didn't know if I ever could. Or would want to.

19

A few weeks after getting back from Mexico, Mago said, "Gaby and I are looking for an apartment together."

"Really?" I asked, looking away from the TV, where I was watching *Anne of Green Gables* on the Disney Channel. "You aren't leaving me, are you?"

She shook her head and threw a pillow at me. "How can you think that? Of course I'll take you with me. We can leave here and finally be in a place where we can be happy."

I threw the pillow back at her so she wouldn't see how relieved I was. I knew she'd forgiven me for the fight between us in Mexico. She'd said she understood, but for a second I'd thought she was going to tell me she was leaving without me.

I turned back to the TV and continued to follow Anne Shirley on her adventures. I wanted to be like Anne: strong, adventurous, pretty, and smart. I wanted to have her imagination and her way with words. But most of all, I wanted to live in a beautiful place like she did. Anne had lost her parents when she was a baby, and as a little orphan, her childhood had been very difficult. But Anne got lucky when she was adopted by people who let her be who she wanted to be, who loved her and praised her for her talents, and who were not afraid to tell her they were proud of her.

Sometimes I imagined getting adopted too, by someone who would be proud of my accomplishments. Like my latest one—being chosen to be the assistant drum major of Franklin's marching band! I'd designed the field formations to the music Mr. Quan had chosen for us to learn. I'd led the band to place second in a competition held at Wilson High School. I'd led the band at the Highland Park Christmas Parade on Figueroa Street. Even though the parade route was only a ten-minute walk from my house, my father hadn't come to see me march.

I was jealous of Anne because, unlike me, she had people who noticed even her smallest accomplishments.

The weeks passed with no news about an apartment. That spring semester I enrolled in track and field. I didn't really like running, but Mago did. On the weekends we would go to Franklin to jog around the football field, and she'd leave me in the dust. I thought that if I practiced every day at school, I would get faster so that I could keep up with my sister. So far, track and field hadn't made me faster, but it had gotten me a boyfriend!

His name was Steve, and he had hazel eyes and

dimples in his cheeks. If Mago rented an apartment too far from Franklin, I knew I'd have to transfer and never see Steve or Franklin again, never mind that I was in my last semester there. I'd follow my Mago to the end of the Earth if I had to. And I'd give up Steve, no matter how cute he was.

A week later, while we were getting ready for bed, Mago said she and Gaby had found an apartment in La Habra. I didn't know where that was, and how far from school it was, but before I could tell her that anywhere was fine with me, she said, "Nena, I won't be able to take you with me."

I sat down on my bed and looked down at my feet, not knowing what to say. I thought about my Quinceañera, about receiving Holy Communion when I wasn't supposed to. *Here it is. Judgment Day. Please, don't take away my Mago, God. Punish me in another way, if you must. But don't take her from me.*

"Why?" was all I managed to say.

"The manager doesn't allow extra people in the apartment. Gaby already has her son, and her aunt is also going to be living with us to babysit. With me that makes four."

"But I could share a room with you, just like we've always done."

"I know, but they won't allow more than four people in the apartment." She stood up from her bed and came to sit

275

with me. "Besides, Nena, you have two and a half months to go before you finish high school. It wouldn't be right to pull you out now and transfer you to another school. I'm sorry, Nena. I really wanted to take you with me."

"Then stay," I said, clutching her hand. "Like you said, I'm almost done with school. In June I could start looking for a job, and we can rent a place together."

She shook her head. "I can't stand being here anymore. I feel that I'm going to go crazy. I want to live my life in peace. Do what I want without having to explain anything to anyone."

I thought about her new boyfriend, Victor, whom she'd met at work. I knew she hated that Papi didn't let her go out much. Now that Carlos was married and had left home, Papi had been even more vigilant with us girls. I knew Victor was one of the reasons why Mago was so desperate to get out. Like Carlos, she was also in love, too in love to put up with our father's restrictions and house rules. But how could she not wait for me to graduate so we could leave together?

She put her arm around me, and we stayed like that for a long time. She didn't say when she was leaving, and I didn't ask. I kept hoping that maybe, just maybe, things would change.

A few days later I knew it was for real when Mago broke the news to Papi. "You're such an ungrateful daughter!" he yelled. "After everything I've done for you, this is how

276

you repay me?" He said she just wanted to be able to go out with as many men as she wanted without anyone telling her what's right or wrong. He banged his fists on the table and stood up. "If you leave this house, you'll be dead to me. I won't ever want to see you again."

Mago didn't say anything. We stayed there at the kitchen table long after Papi had left.

"Stay with us, Mago," I said, grabbing her hand. "Stay with *me*."

Every day I'd come home from school, wondering if that was the day when she'd leave. But in the evening Mago would come home like she always had. Papi didn't talk to her, but by the second week it was as if nothing had happened. Mago didn't bring up the subject anymore, and Papi ended the silent treatment. All of us even went out to dinner at Papi's favorite restaurant—La Perla in East LA—when I received the best news ever. I'd been accepted to UC Irvine!

"I'm so proud of you, Nena," Mago said to me, reaching to grab my hand from across the restaurant table.

"Me too," Carlos said. Papi didn't say anything like that, but the fact that he'd taken us to his favorite restaurant said a lot, especially because he hardly ever took us anywhere. We sat there and listened to the mariachi, and I sang along with them. Papi sang along to "Volver, Volver." I looked at his smile, and I smiled too. Nothing made him happier than to listen to the songs of

Vicente Fernández. Mago, Carlos, and I sang along, and I got lost in the beauty of the murals at La Perla. This was how I wanted my family to be, always together.

Two days later I came home to an empty bedroom.

All of my sister's clothes were gone, all except for a pair of overall shorts I'd often borrowed from her. A farewell present? I dropped onto her bed and sat there for a long time. I couldn't believe she'd left without telling me good-bye. Mami had left with the wrestler without saying good-bye too. Just like our mother, Mago hadn't wanted to see my tears. Maybe she thought it was better this way. But I didn't think coming home to an empty closet was better than saying good-bye and watching her go out the door.

I heard the front door open and close. My father was home, and I'd not done my chores. I rushed to the kitchen to wash the dishes. My hands shook as I picked them up to lather them. My eyes burned from crying.

He came into the kitchen and grabbed a beer, not saying anything to me. I was used to him ignoring me. And honestly, I preferred that to when he did pay attention, because it was only to insult me or reprimand me for something or other. But that day I knew I had to break the silence. I just didn't know how to tell him Mago was gone. I waited until he took a drink from his beer, and right before he disappeared into his bedroom, I blurted out the news.

"Mago has left," I said.

"What?" He turned to look at me. I shut off the faucet and dried my hands.

"She's gone."

He headed to my bedroom and stood there in the middle, just like I'd done earlier. He looked at the empty closet, the empty dresser drawers, at Mago's posters on the wall, the only reminder that she'd once lived there.

"You're not allowed to see your sister anymore," he said. "If she wants to leave, so be it. But you," he said as he pointed a finger at me, "will have nothing to do with her."

What did he mean by that? I didn't understand.

"After everything I've done for her, *this* is how she repays me?" he asked. I stood frozen in place. My fear kept my mouth shut. "If she wants to go and live a corrupted life, then she's dead to me," he said. He talked about Carlos, about how disappointed he was in him, and now in Mago. He looked at me and shook his head. He looked at me as if I'd disappointed him too, though I was still there, with him.

I wanted to tell him I'd be different, that I'd seen with my own eyes the poverty he'd helped us escape. I'd seen with my own eyes the reason he'd been such a tyrant about school. I wanted to tell him I'd do what Mago and Carlos hadn't been able to do. I would go to UC Irvine and get my degree. I would be somebody he could be proud of.

But he said to me, "You can forget all about going to that university. You're going to be a failure too, just like them, so don't even bother." Then he walked away.

"No, Papi, please!" I begged. But he slammed his bedroom door shut.

I returned to my room. A room that was now only mine. *He wasn't serious,* I told myself. *He's just angry with Mago and will change his mind tomorrow. He knows how important this is for me, for the family. He will let me go.* I walked to my sister's twin bed, got under the covers, and buried my nose in the pillow, trying to drown myself in her favorite scent—Beautiful, by Estée Lauder. I thought about Abuelita Chinta, my mother, and now my sister. The void inside me became bigger and bigger as I realized that the women I loved most were far from me.

20

Now that Mago and Carlos were gone, the three-bedroom apartment felt too empty. My father moved us to the two-bedroom unit upstairs and rented the three-bedroom unit to my cousin Lola and her family. He bought me a full-size bed and got rid of the two twin-size beds Mago and I had slept in. I was glad of that. It was easier to deal with my sister's absence now that I didn't have to look at her empty bed. All traces that I'd once shared a room with my sister were gone. Now this room was mine alone.

I had no one left but Steve. I didn't need to sneak behind my father's back anymore to have a boyfriend. I told him about Steve because I didn't care what Papi would do anymore. He had taken Mago away. He'd taken UC Irvine away. What else could he take away from me?

Surprisingly enough, he allowed me to have a boyfriend. He said I was seventeen now, a young woman. He said, "Just be careful and don't embarrass me."

My father's permission to have a boyfriend gave me

hope. If I could convince him about that, could I convince him to let me see Mago again?

Prom was in a few weeks and Mago was taking me shopping. I wanted to ask my father for permission to see my sister, but just when I was about to ask him, I'd change my mind. If he said no, I wouldn't get a dress. If I didn't have a dress, I couldn't go to prom. So I didn't risk it.

I snuck out of the house to meet Mago in the alley nearby. I told Papi I was going jogging at Sycamore Grove Park. That was one advantage of signing up for track and field. I had an excuse to get out of the house. Mago took me to the mall to pick out a prom dress.

I was happy to see my sister and happy to be doing something that sisters do all the time together—shopping. For a moment I forgot I wasn't supposed to be there. For a moment it felt like old times, just me and my sister. I felt like a normal teenage girl whose only worry was what to wear to prom.

"It's so good to see you, Nena," Mago said. "I miss you."

"I do too," I said.

I tried on dress after dress, but Mago shook her head and brought me more. I'd never tried on so many dresses in my life! "You look fat. You look short. Your skin looks too yellow. Yuck, you look like an old lady!" she'd say with every dress.

Finally I tried on a wine-colored dress made of crushed velvet with a long slit on the side. Nothing fancy because

Mago was the one paying for it, and I didn't want her to spend too much money. It was a simple dress, but the deep red color went well with my olive skin and black hair.

She took me home and dropped me off in the alley half a block away from the house. "I'll come on prom day and help you get ready, okay?" she said.

"Okay. Thanks for the dress, Mago. You're the best," I said, hugging her. I looked around, making sure Papi wasn't spying on me. He'd kill me if he saw me. Or worse, he wouldn't let me go to prom.

"He'll change his mind eventually," she said. "He can't keep us separated like this. I don't want to be sneaking around like a criminal. You're my sister. I have rights."

"I hope so," I said. I walked home, thinking about the many times I'd asked him for permission to see her. He'd always said no.

The day of the prom, as promised, Mago came in the afternoon to help me get ready. Papi was watching TV. I asked Mila to tell him I'd gone to the store to buy hair spray, if he asked. She knew Mago was waiting for me, and I was glad she understood. This was a big day for me. I needed my sister.

I met Mago in the alley again. She'd brought all her hair supplies and makeup. We moved to the backseat of her car. She did my hair first, and soon she got impatient. "I can't believe I have to do this in a car!" she said as she struggled to access all sides of my head. She tried to work quickly because we knew that once my dad realized I wasn't home, he'd start asking questions.

When she put hair spray on, I got dizzy. We had to open the doors to let all the fumes out. "Hurry," I said, biting my nails, imagining my father calling out my name, knocking, and then opening the door and noticing that I wasn't in my room. And what if Mila told him where I was? Not going to prom was the worst thing that could happen! For the first time I felt like a normal girl doing what girls do here in America.

"There," she said. "That's the best I can do for now."

I looked in the rearview mirror. My hair was pulled back from my face and up in a bun. There were two braids on either side that twisted around the bun in an intricate design. "Wow. You can do miracles," I said.

"Okay, now your makeup. Quick."

I liked this part because now I could look at her. She was only inches from me, and I got to study every bit of her face. I admired and envied her long eyelashes, her narrow face that always made her look thinner in photographs. Whereas my wide, round face always made me look thirty pounds heavier. I looked at her scars. The one on her eyelid looked like miniature train tracks. The scars weren't very noticeable, and they didn't make her any less pretty. It was sad that whenever she looked at herself in the mirror, to her they were big and ugly.

"Keep still, Nena," she said as she applied mascara.

I couldn't stop blinking. Applying mascara always made me nervous.

"Hurry," I said. "I'm going to get caught."

When she was finished, I didn't have time to look in the mirror. I got out of the car and started running out of the alley. "Thank you!" I yelled. Wait. I hadn't even said bye! I ran back again, gave her a big hug, and then darted away.

"Have fun!" she said. I slowed down when I got near the house, making sure my dad wasn't anywhere outside. Mrs. Giuliano was sitting at her window. She waved at me, and I wondered if she'd seen me with Mago. She wouldn't tell on me, would she?

I made my way upstairs, and luckily, only Mila was in the kitchen. She said my dad was in the bedroom. "How is she?" she asked.

"Fine," I said. I rushed to my room, hoping my dad wouldn't open the door to his bedroom at that very moment. I made it safely into my room and looked at myself in the mirror. It always amazed me how good my sister was at styling hair and applying makeup. The girl looking back at me wasn't me. It was a pretty version of me, one that my sister had created. At that moment I felt almost as pretty as her. She'd done my makeup exactly the way she did hers. When I looked in the mirror, it was almost as if I were seeing her looking back at me.

I carefully wiped away the beads of perspiration that had gathered on my upper lip on my run to the house. I didn't have much makeup of my own, so I was careful not to wipe too hard. My pretty face had to last me the whole night.

I put on my burgundy dress and my heels, and patted my bun once more as I waited for Steve. I knew it was silly, but I felt that I was taking Mago along with me to prom.

Steve showed up in his mother's beat-up car the color of baby vomit. He had promised me a white Corvette, and I had pictured him picking me up looking like a knight on a white horse.

"My neighbor didn't let me borrow his Corvette after all," he said. "You look beautiful! Wow."

"Thanks to my sister!" I whispered.

Mila came out and took pictures of us before we left. Steve held me tight. He couldn't keep his eyes off me. My dad didn't leave his room. It was my prom night, but to him there was nothing special about it. So I left without him saying bye to me.

Steve opened the car door for me, and I couldn't stop laughing about it. That was the first time anyone had opened the door for me, like men did in those black-and-white movies I watched on AMC. I felt like Katharine Hepburn, and I pretended he was Cary Grant. Steve looked just as gorgeous in his black tuxedo and bow tie. And I was crazy about his hazel eyes and dimples.

Even though the car was a hundred years old and rattled, sending puffs of smoke into the air as Steve and I made our way down the street, I pretended we were in the Corvette.

At the prom all my friends praised my makeup and hair, and they wanted to know which beauty salon I'd gone to. I didn't tell them I'd gotten my hair done in a car parked in an alley that stank of pee and was littered with trash. I did tell them it had been my sister who'd fixed me up.

"Lucky you," they said.

Steve and I danced for hours. I didn't want the night to end. I wanted to stay there in his arms, on that beautiful dance floor with crystal chandeliers and disco lights.

After prom was over, Steve wanted us to go to the beach with his friends. But the car wouldn't start! Steve tried over and over again, but nothing. He popped the hood and looked in there, but he didn't know how to fix a car and there was nothing he could do but look.

"I think it's your battery," one of the valet drivers told us.

We got someone to jump-start the car, and we sat there in the parking lot, watching Steve's friends start to drive off one by one to the beach.

"Well," he said, "should we risk it?"

"What if it dies again?" I said. I felt like Cinderella. My chariot was turning back into a pumpkin! "If I don't get home on time, my father will kill me."

When we got to my house, Steve didn't turn off the car because he was afraid it might not start again. So he walked me to the door and gave me a quick kiss and left. The house was dark and quiet. Papi and Mila were asleep. There was no one there to ask me how my prom had gone.

In my room I stood before the mirror. My hair was still perfect. My makeup was still beautiful. In the reflection, I could see my sister looking back at me. I heard her asking me how it had gone. "It was great," I said. "Magical."

21

In June, I became the third person in my family to graduate from high school. Though I was proud of that small accomplishment, it was a bittersweet day for me. It was painful to hear my peers talking about their plans after graduation, such as preparing for going off to college, knowing that I might not be going anywhere if I couldn't convince Papi to allow me to go to UCI. It was also painful to see my family split in half at the Occidental College amphitheater, where the graduation was held. Mago and Carlos sat on one side of the theater, and Papi sat on the opposite side because he still refused to have anything to do with Mago. Mila hadn't bothered coming, and neither had my mother.

When I was called up to receive my diploma, I didn't know which side of the amphitheater to look at—to the left, where my siblings sat, or to the right, where my father sat. As I shook my principal's hand, I kept my eyes looking neither to the right nor the left but straight ahead—at the faces of strangers.

*   *   *

My graduation came and went, and true to his word, Papi wouldn't allow me to send in my paperwork to UC Irvine, and since I was still underage, it required his personal and tax information, and his signature, which he refused to give me. I was too much of a coward to falsify his signature. I was too much of a coward to fight him on it. I fought him instead about Mago. I couldn't win two fights. But maybe I might win the one that mattered to me most. Papi threatened to beat me if I dared to step out of the house to go see her. I hoped that with time he'd change his mind about that, too.

Then the news broke that Carlos's wife was pregnant, and a month later Mago confessed that she, too, was expecting. That pushed my father over the edge. And it terrified me to the core. Now that Mago was going to have her own baby to hold and cherish, there wouldn't be room for me in her life.

"You'll always be my Nena," Mago said to me over the phone. When I didn't say anything, she said, "I'm going to go pick you up and take you somewhere. You tell our father that I'm going to go visit you and that he can't do anything about it."

"You know he'll get angry," I said.

"Who cares?" she said. "I'm sick of this. I won't hide anymore, and neither will you. Or are you ashamed of me now?"

"Of course not," I said. "Fine, I'll do it. I'll tell him he can't stop me from seeing you."

Throughout the week there were times when I approached my father to tell him Mago was coming to pick me up on Sunday and I was going out with her whether he liked it or not. But just as I was about to say that, I'd choke up with fear and turn around and go back to my room.

That summer his drinking had gotten worse. Lately I'd been waking to the sound of a beer can being opened. My father now drank before he left for work. And when he returned, he drank all evening before going to bed. He argued with Mila over everything. Even about her weekly visits to her children. "Your place is here, at home," he'd tell her.

"I won't stop seeing my kids or my family," she'd say.

My father hated Mila's family because they had never accepted him. They had always blamed him for breaking up Mila's first marriage. He thought she was being disloyal to him by going over there to see them. Although I'd never seen him hit Mila, there were times when I could almost see the urge inside him. Those times he would hit me instead.

True to her word, Mago came over on Sunday. I told Mila that Mago was downstairs, and Mila didn't think it was a good idea. "Your dad's going to get mad," she said as I headed to their bedroom and knocked.

When he didn't open the door, I mustered the nerve to open the door myself. He was sitting on a chair looking out the window with a beer in his hand. I went in with hesitant steps. This was foreign territory for me. I'd never been allowed to spend time in their bedroom. He was listening to his favorite song by Los Tigres del Norte, "La Jaula de Oro."

Even though the music wasn't loud, he acted as if he hadn't heard me come in.

"What do you want?" he said when I came to stand beside him.

"Mago is downstairs. She wants to take me out."

"Tell her to leave," he said. "I already told you I don't want her coming here. I don't want her seeing you."

"But she's my sister!"

"She chose to leave, didn't she? If she really cared about you, she wouldn't have left."

I started to cry then, like I always did with him. He always knew how to say things that would hurt me to the core. I hated crying. I hated letting him see how much power he had over me, to make me cry just like that, not even having laid a finger on me. "She's my sister and I want to see her," I said.

"I already told you no!" he yelled.

I started walking away, determined to disobey him. "Well, I'm going anyway. She's all I have, and you can't keep me away from her!"

"Reyna," he yelled just as I got to the door. I stopped and looked at him. "If you go out with her, don't you ever come back here."

292

"Fine!"

I rushed out of the room, past the dining room, the kitchen, out the back door. *This is what I needed! Now that he's kicked me out, Mago will be forced to take me with her. I can finally be with her!* I was halfway down the stairs and could see Mago's car parked in front of the apartments. Suddenly I felt as if my hair was tearing out of my scalp. "You aren't going anywhere!" Papi yelled, yanking my hair so hard that I fell over backward. I held on to my hair. He tightened his grip and dragged me up the stairs. I started screaming for Mago, feeling as if my entire scalp was coming off. The last thing I saw before he dragged me into the apartment was Mago getting out of the car.

"Mago! Mago!" I yelled over and over again. My father slammed me against the kitchen wall and beat me with his fists. Mila stood by the door of the living room, as always, not doing anything to help me. "Get my sister," I yelled to her. "Get my sister!" She turned and ran out of the house.

The beating continued and his fist connected with my nose. I covered my face, trying to protect myself. Blood soaked into my shirt. *Where is she? Why won't she come and stop him, take me away from him?* "Mago! Mago!" I yelled. There was a rushing in my ears as his fists fell on me, as hard as rocks.

"Stop. Leave her alone!" a voice said. Suddenly the blows stopped.

I opened my eyes. I was on the floor, crying. My father stood above me. Mila walked back into the kitchen. "Where's Mago?" It wasn't Mago's voice I'd heard. "Why won't she come?"

"She left," Mila said.

I shook my head, unable to believe what she'd said. It couldn't be true. *How could Mago have left when she knew he was hitting me? No, no. There has to be a mistake.* "Mago!" I yelled at the top of my lungs. "Mago!"

But no one came.

"Ya ves?" Papi said, wiping my blood from his hand. "You see. That's how much she cares." I looked at the door, waiting for my sister to come, but she didn't. I looked up at my father, at his fists, and at that moment I just wanted him to keep going, to keep beating me and beating me with those hands that were the same shape as my own. Keep beating me until I could no longer think anymore, until those hands made me disappear, cease to exist. *She left. She left. She left.*

He went back to his room with another beer in his hand. Mila helped me stand up.

"You should understand," Mila said to me as I headed to my bedroom. "Your sister is pregnant. If she'd come up here to defend you, who knows what he would have done to her. He could've hurt the baby."

I left her in the kitchen and made my way to my room to lock myself in.

22

My bedroom was my prison.

No, my bedroom was my haven. From the door in, I was safe. From the door out, the demons would come with their mocking faces. I lay in bed and waited for Mila and my dad to turn in for the night. My stomach growled from hunger, but I wouldn't go out. Not until Mila was done cooking, not until she and my father were done eating dinner, watching TV. Not until the door to their bedroom closed with a final click of the lock. When the house was silent and dark, only then did I come out. This was how it'd been since my father had beaten me. I was afraid that if I came out of the room, he'd come down on me like a vulture. Little by little he pecked at my soul. I was afraid, sometimes, that one day there would be nothing left.

Finally the television would get shut off. Finally I'd hear their footsteps fading into their bedroom. Finally they would fall asleep. I tiptoed out of the room and rushed to the kitchen to grab whatever Mila had made for dinner. I didn't heat it up. He might come out, and

I didn't want to see him. I gobbled down the food in my room and hid the dirty plate under the bed.

I tossed and turned in bed. I knew sleep wouldn't come. It was yet another thing I had lost. I couldn't remember the last time I'd had a good night's sleep. I lay awake, wondering what Mago was doing, what Carlos was doing, what my mother was doing. All three of them had someone to be with, while I was here, in my room. Alone.

I turned on the TV and kept the volume as low as possible. I stuffed the cracks in the door so my father wouldn't see the light from the TV. This was as close as I could come to making myself disappear from his sight.

Then I discovered my hero, there on the TV. Dr. Sam Beckett. He traveled in time to fix the lives of other people on a show called *Quantum Leap*. Oh, how I wished Sam Beckett could jump into my life! Could come and live it for me. Make things right in a way I could not. In a way I might never be able to. But in the real world there are no heroes.

Then one day I realized that if I didn't like where I was, I needed to figure out a way to change it. I realized there was only one person who could get me out of that hole.

Me.

When my father came home from work, I didn't hide in my bedroom. Instead I went out to the kitchen, where he was sitting down to drink his beer. I took a deep breath and said, "Tomorrow I'm going to Pasadena City College to enroll." I waited for him to say no. I was ready for a fight. But my father looked at me, and whatever it was he saw in my eyes made him keep quiet. I turned around, and as I headed back to my room, he stopped me.

"You know, Chata, when my father took me to the fields to work, my job was to guide the oxen in a straight line. My father gave me a stick and said that if the oxen didn't listen to me, to hit them as hard as I could. I was nine years old, Chata. Do you understand?"

I took a deep breath, unable to say anything. He was telling me he'd learned violence as a child. Violence was the only inheritance his parents had given him. I wanted to say something. I was still too angry to forgive what he'd done to me, but I wanted to understand what he was trying to tell me. But too soon he had turned away from me. Too soon he was opening the refrigerator door, taking out another Budweiser, and I knew that the father who had spoken just a minute before was gone.

Not wasting any time, I quickly enrolled at PCC. I still couldn't believe I'd stood up to my father, that I'd given him no choice but to say yes. He wouldn't help me, though, not financially, not emotionally, not the way he had helped Mago and Carlos. It hurt me to know it was he who had given me the dream of having a college education, and yet it was he who was now standing in my way. But I wouldn't let him.

297

I enrolled in an English class that was a requirement to transfer to a four-year college. My teacher was Diana Savas. When I walked into the classroom, I thought she was Latina. She had short black hair and brown eyes framed by glasses. It turned out that she was Greek American, but, to my surprise, she spoke excellent Spanish! I liked her right away. That a non-Latina had taken the time to learn my native tongue impressed me.

In the second week of class, Dr. Savas assigned us an expository essay about the groups to which we belonged (racial, economic, religious groups, etc.). I went home to work on my essay, but it was hard to write. What group did I belong to? I had no idea. I'd never thought of myself as belonging anywhere outside my family. So that was what I wrote, about my family and the place I had come from.

A few days after turning in my essay, Dr. Savas asked me to come to her office. "You wrote an autobiographical essay," she said. "I need you to do the essay again, but," she added, "I think you're a very good writer."

"You do?" I asked, surprised. No teacher had ever told me I was a good writer. Ever since I'd won that writing competition in eighth grade, I'd been writing here and there, mostly short stories and cheesy love poems. But I'd never thought I was very good, and no one had ever said so.

When Dr. Savas handed me back my paper, I felt different somehow. "Yes, I think you are very talented," she said.

When the semester ended, I passed the class with an A, but I was sad that I'd no longer have Dr. Savas as a teacher. I went home on my last day of class, still thinking about her. Without giving myself a break to celebrate that I'd just finished my first college class, I pulled out my notebook and started writing another story.

23

When the fall semester began, I stopped by Dr. Savas's office to say hello. It was my nineteenth birthday that day, and I shyly mentioned it to her because there was no one to celebrate my birthday with. Dr. Savas picked up a book she had on her desk and said, "I went to see a panel of Latino writers this weekend and bought this book. I think you'll like it." She handed it to me, and I looked down at the cover to read the title. *The Moths and Other Stories*, by Helena María Viramontes. I'd never heard of it before. Latino literature wasn't something I was familiar with.

"I want you to have it," she said with a smile. She took the book from me and wrote *Happy Birthday, Reynita* on the title page and handed it back. No one had ever called me Reynita. Not even my mother.

"Thank you," I said. This was the very first book I'd ever been given. One that I could keep and not have to return to the library.

I went home and read *The Moths*. For the first time

since I'd become an avid reader, I found myself reading about characters who lived in a world like my own, characters with the same color skin as mine. With the same heartaches and dreams.

As the weeks went by, I visited Dr. Savas—or Diana, as she said to call her—at her office between classes. I never told her about life at home. We talked instead about books and writing. She was always asking me about my latest story, my latest poem. Sometimes I wanted to tell her about all the problems at home, about the increasing arguments between Mila and my father. Lately they'd been fighting over a woman. Mila thought my father was cheating on her with someone at work. He denied it. I heard them yelling in their bedroom. When I got home from school, they would be in the living room, screaming at each other. I'd walk by them and head to my bedroom. It was better if I stayed out of their way and didn't take sides, but I couldn't help thinking that now Mila knew how my mother had felt when my father had been cheating on her with Mila.

One day I heard Mila screaming. That weekend Betty, who was thirteen, had come over. Mila screamed again, and Betty and I went running to the living room, just in time to see our father shoving Mila onto the couch. He fell on top of her and began to beat her. Mila squirmed beneath him, but she wasn't able to get him off her. I stood there, not able to move or speak. I opened my mouth, but nothing came out. I couldn't believe he was hitting her. All those years *I'd* been on the receiving end of his fists. Not her. Never her. Betty looked at me, wanting me to do something. I put my arm around her and pulled her close. I wished she wasn't seeing this. I wished I hadn't brought her over that day.

Mila finally got my father off her. "Leave me alone!" she yelled. She ran out the door, down the stairs. He followed behind her, cussing at her. Then I heard the sound of metal falling, and my stepmother crying out. "Natalio. Stop it! Stop it!" I heard my cousin Lola and her husband yelling at my father to stop from the floor below us.

When Betty and I rushed downstairs, Mila was sobbing in Lola's arms, and my father was being restrained by Lola's husband, Chente. My father broke loose of Chente's grasp, and for a second it seemed as if he were going to pounce on Mila again. Instead he rushed toward the stairs. It took me a second to realize he was heading my way, and I quickly moved myself and Betty out of the way to let him pass. I was so relieved when he didn't glance at us. He just went into the apartment without a word.

Mila's leg was bleeding. My father had pushed her onto the garden tools under the stairwell, and she'd cut herself on the spikes of the rake.

"Come on, Mila. You need to go to the hospital," Lola said. Her husband helped Mila to the car, and I stood there not knowing what to do. *Should I go with her? Should I stay with him?*

"Stay with my uncle," Lola said, making the decision for me. "Go keep an eye on him."

I stood there on the first step, and I couldn't get myself to take the next step up to go back to the apartment. Betty and I looked at each other, not knowing what to do. I didn't know how to be a little mother to my sister.

"Jeez," Betty said, shaking her head at what had just happened.

Eventually I found the courage to take Betty and myself back upstairs. We went through the back door and tiptoed across the kitchen, and I poked my head into the living room. My father had turned off the light, and he was sitting there on the couch, motionless. I wondered if he had fallen asleep. We went into my room and stayed there.

I woke up to someone shaking me. I opened my eyes, and I saw a female police officer standing over me. She shone a flashlight into my eyes. "What's going on?" I said.

She took me and Betty into the living room, where two other police officers were putting handcuffs on my father. He didn't look at me and Betty. He never looked up from the floor. Then they walked him out the door. I watched them make their way down the stairs. I couldn't take my eyes off the handcuffs. I couldn't believe my father was in handcuffs. I looked at Betty, wishing once again she wasn't there to see him like this. My mother was always telling her bad things about him, so she didn't like him very much to begin with. What would she think of him now, at seeing her father turned into a criminal?

When they put him in the patrol car, he looked up at us for a brief moment before the car door closed and they took him away.

"Let's go inside," the female cop said. We sat in the living room. "Can you tell me everything that happened?"

I found that I couldn't speak. How could I tell her about the abuse? How could I tell her I was ashamed of what he'd done, that as his daughter I shared in his guilt? How could I say that even though I knew he was getting what he deserved, I was still afraid for him? I didn't want anything to happen to him. I didn't want him to go to jail. *What's going to happen to him?* I wanted to ask her. *To me? To us all?*

To my surprise, when I dropped off Betty, my mother offered to take me in. I decided to move in with her because I knew I couldn't be at my father's apartment anymore. Mila had returned from the hospital black-and-blue from head to toe. It shamed me to look at her. She knew I'd said nothing, done nothing, to defend her.

I took my few belongings to my mother's little apartment. That night I slept on the floor, wedged against the dining table. My mother, Betty, and Leonardo slept sideways on the bed, with their feet hanging over the edge. Rey slept on the floor, right against the entertainment center. If I reached out, I could almost touch him. That was how small the room was.

By the second night, I knew I couldn't stay there. My last class at PCC ended at seven p.m. It'd take me nearly three hours to get to my mother's house, from Pasadena all the way to downtown LA riding the bus. It was almost ten when I found myself walking alone down 7th Street. Homeless people slept on the sidewalks, and I had to step over them. Drunks pushed their shopping carts. Men drove by and whistled at me. I walked so fast that my side was hurting, my legs were burning. When a group of men turned the corner and started heading toward me, I took off running and didn't look back.

"Why don't you drop that last class?" my mother said when I got home. I tried to catch my breath, but it was coming in gasps. I shook my head, horrified at her suggestion. *That is how it starts,* I wanted to tell her. *Once you drop one class, it makes it easier to drop them all.*

I visited Diana during her office hours. I needed someone to talk to, and she was the only person I could trust. I knocked on her office door, and for a moment I thought about turning around and leaving. *Why should I burden someone else with my worries?* As soon as she opened the door and said "Reynita!" in that high-pitched voice of hers, I knew I'd made the right decision to come to her.

I told Diana what had happened over the weekend and the past three days that I'd been at my mother's. I couldn't stop the tears from coming even though I told myself not to cry. Diana didn't need my drama. I didn't want to burden her with my problems. Diana grabbed my hand and said, "Reynita, you can't be in that situation any longer. You have to think about school. That's all you should worry about." I wiped the tears from my eyes. How could I not worry? How could I escape all of this? I had nowhere to go.

"Would you like to come stay at my house?" Diana asked.

"What?" I asked, rubbing my eyes.

"I live across the street from here in a house owned by PCC, and it's got three bedrooms."

"But, Diana, I don't want to trouble you with all my problems. I just couldn't—" I stopped myself, took a deep breath, and then mustered up the nerve to say what was really on my mind. "Yes, I'll go with you, Diana."

"From now on, Reynita, my home will be your home," she said.

As Diana held my hand, I realized I had been wrong— there are heroes in real life.

24

Diana was from the Midwest and was thirty-eight years old. She'd come out to Los Angeles to get her PhD at UCLA. She had been a starving student. She had no family in Los Angeles and had forged her way alone. Diana later told me that I had reminded her of herself—a young woman trying to find her way in this big city, all alone, but with a huge desire to succeed. It was that, and the thought of me walking the dark streets of Skid Row if I'd stayed with my mother, that had made Diana want to take me in.

Mila didn't press charges, and my father returned home. They told me I could go back, but I knew I couldn't. I shouldn't. Something told me things were only going to get worse between them. I left them to fight their own battles. I was glad my father was not in trouble with the law, but at the same time I was disappointed in Mila for dropping the charges and staying. I'd thought she was a different kind of woman.

At first it was awkward for me to be in Diana's house. My instinct was to lock myself up in the guest room and keep out of her way, give her as little trouble as possible. At my father's house I'd learned to be invisible. But Diana wasn't my father. She refused to let me disappear. She coaxed me out of the room a few days later. She wouldn't allow me to hide in my room. She wouldn't ignore me.

"Join me in the living room, Reynita," she said. Since I didn't want her to mistake my survival skills for ungratefulness, I accepted her invitation.

I found myself sitting in the living room in the safety of Diana's house, and it was a rare feeling, to be out in the living room and not be afraid that someone would yell at me, beat me, or put me down. Diana graded papers, and I did my homework while listening to melancholic Greek music. I didn't understand the words, but the rhythm reminded me of romantic Mexican songs.

Diana wasn't married and didn't have children, but she had four small dogs who kept her company, whom she'd rescued from the streets. The third bedroom had been converted into a library, and she had shelves and shelves full of books. So many books that they spilled into the living room. I'd never been in a house with books. I thought I was in heaven. During a break from grading she went into that room and came back with a book. She handed it to me and said, "Here, have you read this?"

I took the book from her and read the title, *The House on Mango Street*. I shook my head. I'd never even heard of Sandra Cisneros.

"Reynita, you have to read this book. It's wonderful."

I grabbed the book and found a comfortable spot on the couch, where I read *The House on Mango Street* while Diana graded papers. It's difficult to describe the impact this book had on me. It was absolutely beautiful. Exquisite. I was in awe of the poetic language, the beautiful images, the way the words just flowed together. But there was more to the book than Cisneros's writing talent that made me love it. When I got to the chapter titled "Sally," I broke down. I shook with an intense sadness and helplessness and cried. This chapter was about a young girl who lived with an abusive father. Every day she rushed home after school, and then she couldn't come out. *Sally, do you sometimes wish you didn't have to go home? Do you wish your feet would one day keep walking and take you far away from Mango Street, far away . . .*

How did Cisneros know this was exactly how I'd felt for so many years? Just wishing my feet could keep walking, keep walking to another place, to a beautiful home where I was loved and wanted. I reread the chapter, and with every word I felt Cisneros reaching out and talking to me. I felt a connection to this author, this woman, whom I'd never met. Suddenly I wanted to meet her and ask her, *How did you know? How did you know this is how I felt?*

"You need to write, Reynita," Diana said to me every day. She gave me other books written by Latina authors— Isabel Allende, Julia Alvarez, and Laura Esquivel. Latina writers who were writing about the things I liked to write about. I began to understand why Diana had been telling me I should be a writer. I hadn't been exposed to Chicano/Latino literature before. I'd spent too many years reading Sweet Valley High, Stephen King novels, and cheesy Harlequin romances. I could have been reading something more powerful, more meaningful. But I hadn't even known, until then, that Chicano/Latino literature existed.

Those books, like *The House on Mango Street*, proved a revelation. There were people out there who understood, who had experienced the things I was going through. Diana planted a seed inside me, and through those books the seed began to grow. She exposed me to things I'd never experienced before. She took me to Greek and Italian restaurants, teaching me about other cultures besides my own. She showed me foreign films, and sometimes in the evening we sat in her backyard and planned my future while throwing balls for her four dogs to catch.

One day I heard about a writing competition, and at Diana's encouragement I decided to enter. I rewrote the essay I'd written in her class, and with her help I polished it and made it better. I placed second and won one hundred dollars!

"You have to be a writer, Reynita," Diana said to me. "You have to transfer to a good school, Reynita." Over and over she repeated this like a chant. "If Alvarez, Cisneros, and Viramontes can publish their stories, so can you, Reynita."

I didn't know what the future held for me. All I could do back then was allow myself to dream.

25

A year and a half later, when I was in my last semester at PCC, Mila left my father.

Carlos said, "Reyna, you have to go back home. He needs you."

"He's never needed anyone," I said. The thought that my father actually needed me was preposterous to me. The thought of going back there made me sick.

A few days later Carlos called me again. "He tried to kill himself," he said.

"I don't believe you," I said. I didn't believe for a second that my father would commit suicide because a woman had left him.

"He needs someone there to keep an eye on him," Carlos said. "I can't do it. Mago can't do it either. We both work. You have to go back."

I hung up the phone, and for the rest of the day I couldn't stop thinking about my father. In my mind I saw him on the floor with a bullet hole in his head. What if Carlos was right? What if he was trying to hurt himself?

What if, for the first time, he really did need me?

I returned to my father's side because I felt obligated to do so. The spring semester at PCC had ended, graduation had passed, and at the end of the summer I would be heading north to study at UC Santa Cruz, the school I had chosen based on Diana's recommendation. I didn't want to go up north with a guilty conscience. I wanted to go there and have a fresh start.

When I got to his house, my father was sitting at the dining table by himself. It was dinnertime now, but he was sitting at the table in the dark as if waiting for his meal, as if he'd forgotten that Mila was no longer there to cook for him as she had always done. He played with his empty beer can and looked up when I came in. I was shocked at seeing him so thin, so haggard, and his hair full of gray.

"I'm back," I said. He looked surprised, and I wondered if Carlos hadn't told him I was coming back. I asked him if he was hungry, if he wanted me to cook something. He didn't answer me. I opened the refrigerator, but it was almost empty, and my heart started to race because I didn't know how to cook. All those years, Mila had ruled the kitchen and hadn't taught me or Mago how to handle ourselves in the kitchen.

I turned to look at him and found him staring at me. I didn't know if he could see how scared I was of cooking, but he said, "Come on, Chata. Let's get out of here." He pulled his chair back and stood up.

"Where to?" I asked.

"El Pollo Loco," he said. I didn't know what to say. He hated eating out. I loved El Pollo Loco, especially the BRC burrito, so I followed him out the door without complaining. I breathed a sigh of relief, knowing that I wouldn't have to cook for him. When we got to his car, he held up the keys to me.

"Here, you drive."

"Wait—what?" Once in a while Carlos had taken me to practice driving. Mago had tried as well, but she wasn't patient with me at all, especially after I made a dent in her car. I wasn't good enough to drive my father's car. He would criticize my every move. I just knew it. He would probably yell at me or call me a good-for-nothing. "No, you drive."

"Here," he said, and gave me the keys.

I reluctantly took the keys and opened the door. I sat at the wheel and started the car, and then we headed down Granada Street and turned right onto Avenue 52. I drove slowly, carefully, but at the intersection I turned too late and ran the red light. Cars honked at me. Tires screeched. I glanced at my father from the corner of my eye. He was staring straight ahead but said nothing. Thankfully, we got to El Pollo Loco with the car still in one piece.

"I'm sorry," I told him as I gave him back the keys.

"That wasn't bad, Chata," he said.

I didn't know what it was that Mila's departure had done to my father, but he wasn't the same man he'd been before. He was a different father from the one I had come to know. He didn't criticize me. He didn't yell at me. He didn't hit me. He didn't look at me as if I didn't exist. For the first time my father liked having me around.

Mila filed for divorce, and it was a messy process, but I stood by my father during the ordeal and supported him as much as I could. We continued our trips to El Pollo Loco, although sometimes I would cook for him, and he would eat my food without complaining. We would sit in the backyard, where I'd help my father tend the zucchini, corn, peppers, and carrots he'd planted. Sometimes we would sit in the living room and watch the Lakers' game. We would go hiking at Griffith Park. We would go to Sycamore Grove Park and jog until dark. I was so hungry to share with him all the things I had done since I'd moved out of his house. I told him about the English tutoring job I'd gotten at the PCC Learning Center. I told him about joining the Lancer Marching Band and marching in the Rose Parade for the third time. I told him about my stint as a staff writer for the PCC newspaper, and about the time when they had published my article "PCC in the Making," which had taken up the entire page, and how after its publication I'd received a personal letter from the PCC president to congratulate me on it. I told him about the Townsend Press essay competition and other competitions I had entered. I told him about the scholarships I'd gotten to help me pay for UCSC, such as the Hispanic Scholarship Fund. I wanted him to know that even though I'd been apart from him, I still valued what he'd taught me.

"Tell me about your new school," he asked me one day as we were jogging side by side.

So I told him about Santa Cruz, about the redwood trees, the ocean, the literature and writing classes I was going to take there. "Diana said UCSC is a special place. It's a great school for students who are into the arts. She thinks it will help me grow as a writer."

"Six hours is a long drive," he said.

"I'll come visit you every chance I get," I said. "And you can come visit me."

We didn't speak for the remainder of our jog, but my feet felt heavy as I began to wonder if I should stay. How could I leave now, when things were starting to turn around at home, when finally my father was beginning to change? What if I stayed? I'd gotten accepted to UCLA, and even though I'd turned them down for UCSC, couldn't I tell them I'd changed my mind? Wouldn't they take me back?

When I'd picked UCSC, it had been because I'd felt I had no reason to stay in Los Angeles. But now I did have a reason—my father. How could I give him up, now that things were great between us, just when he was finally becoming the father I'd always dreamed he could be?

One night, while we were eating the chiles rellenos I'd made for him, my father put his fork down and looked at me. He said, "I've been talking to Mila."

"About what?" I asked.

"We've decided to work things out. We called the lawyer yesterday and told him to hold off on the divorce."

"What does that mean?"

"It means she's coming back," he said. I forced myself to swallow my food, and I put my fork down. "But there's one condition to her coming back."

"And what's that?"

"She doesn't want you, Mago, or Carlos around."

"And you've agreed?" I asked, feeling the chile relleno burn a hole in my stomach.

My father looked at his plate, not at me. He didn't look at me, not even once. I stood up and went to pack my bags.

26

I went to stay at Diana's house for the remaining days before my departure. She was the last person I saw before I left for Santa Cruz. Edwin, my boyfriend whom I'd met at PCC, picked me up at her house, and there, in her front yard, I said good-bye to her. I waved to her from the car window. As we drove down Colorado Boulevard, I promised myself that one day I would tell everyone about Diana, about this woman who came into my life when I most needed someone, and how she changed it for the better.

Edwin got accepted to California State University Monterey Bay, about an hour south of Santa Cruz. He was majoring in psychology, and this was one of the things I liked most about him, how easy it was to talk to him, how easily he could read me and know the right things to say. On our drive up to Santa Cruz, Edwin said, "Your father is very proud of you, you know?"

I didn't say anything, but his words did ease the pain I felt in my chest as the car sped north, putting mile upon mile between me and my father. I looked out the window, saw the fields stretch out before us as we drove up the 5 North. I thought about my father, about how eighteen years before, he had been working in the fields near here before heading to Los Angeles to try his luck.

"Try to understand him," Edwin said. "He knew you were leaving at the end of the summer. He didn't want to be alone once you left."

"I could have stayed with him," I said.

"He didn't want to hold you back," Edwin said.

When Edwin and I got to UCSC, many students were there already, moving in. I sat in the car with him while I watched students and their parents, grandparents, brothers, and sisters carrying boxes. I saw fathers patting their sons on the back. Mothers crying while clinging to their daughters. "Do you need anything else?" I heard them ask their children. "We will miss you," they said.

I thought of my father and my mother. I thought of Mago, Carlos, and Betty. I wished they were here with me now, sharing this special day with me. But we were three hundred miles apart, and this time it was I who had left.

Edwin helped me take my few belongings to my room. It only took a couple of trips. Then we were done. "Are you going to be okay?" he asked.

"Yeah," I said, although I wasn't so sure.

He pulled out of the parking lot and waved goodbye, promising to come back every weekend to visit me. It made me feel good that he wouldn't be too far, that I would at least have a familiar face to see. I watched him drive away, and as soon as he was out of sight, I went for a walk. It was late afternoon, the sun would be going down, and I wanted to see as much of the campus as I could before it got too dark. As I walked, I immersed myself in the redwood trees, smelling the pungent scent of their needles. I felt all the tension in my body disappear. There was a beauty here I'd never imagined. I heard the wind rustling the trees. I spotted a family of deer, and I stopped and looked at them as they foraged for food. I couldn't believe there were deer here! At the sight of them, I knew I'd made a good choice to leave Los Angeles and come here. I felt like Anne of Green Gables in her Avonlea. Like her, I'd found my perfect place of beauty.

I continued my walk and ended up by Porter College, at the meadow, where I could see the ocean shining blue and streaked with orange. I climbed onto a metal sculpture and I sat there, six feet above the ground. I thought about the first time I'd seen the ocean in Santa Monica. I thought about my father holding my hand, about how afraid I was that he would let go of me.

I looked at the ocean now, and I realized there was no need to be afraid. I'd gotten this far, despite everything. Now all I had to do was focus on what I was there to do— make my dreams a reality. I closed my eyes, and I saw myself at the water's edge, holding tightly to my father's calloused hand.

And I let it go.

EPILOGUE

In June of 1999, I became the first person in my family to graduate from college. At UCSC, I earned my BA in creative writing and film and video, and graduated with college honors, honors in my major, and Phi Beta Kappa. Unlike my high school graduation, this time my whole family was there to celebrate the accomplishment—including my father and my mother!

UCSC has a tradition that seniors are asked to write about a teacher who most inspired them. I wrote about Diana. My essay was chosen as the winner, and Diana was flown up to Santa Cruz to attend my graduation. I gave a speech about her at the ceremony, and that was the first time I ever thanked her publicly for what she had done for me. I haven't stopped talking about her since. I have known Diana for more than twenty years now. She has seen me grow up and turn into the person I am today—a U.S. citizen, a home owner, an author, a wife, and a proud mother of two wonderful children.

I continued my studies and earned an MFA in creative

writing. And, just like Diana and I had once dreamed, I finally met my literary heroes! One day I found myself sitting in Sandra Cisneros's dining room eating carrot cake. I've shared a car ride with Julia Alvarez. I've shared the stage with Helena María Viramontes at a book reading.

Mago, Carlos, Betty, and Leonardo are doing well. My siblings and I continue to support one another as best we can. Between us we have thirteen children! Our goal is to give our children a stable and happy life, and to guide them and help them reach for their dreams.

My relationship with my mother is better now than it's ever been. My siblings and I have done our best to forgive her and accept her for who she is. I now go to Mexico every year with my mother to visit our family there and to give Christmas toys to the children in my old neighborhood. It's one of my favorite things to do with my mother—to visit the country of our birth together.

As for my father, he was diagnosed with liver cancer in 2010. By then my siblings and I had little communication with him. By then he'd managed to chase us away. But I found my way back to my father once again as he fought his battle with cancer. On September 6, 2011, the day before my thirty-sixth birthday, Carlos, Mago, and I found ourselves around his hospital bed listening to the doctor tell us that the hospital had done everything they could for him. I held my father's hand as he took his last breaths.

There were many things I felt that day. I remembered

the difficult moments of my childhood and adolescence with my father. But as I watched him die, I tried to move the bad memories aside, and instead I pulled forth the good memories—the happy moments, such as when he'd returned to Mexico and brought me to the U.S., or when he would sit us down at the kitchen table to tell us about all the dreams he had for us. Or when he and I would jog around the park or tend his vegetable garden. As my father lay dying, I realized that everything I'd gone through with him had shaped the person I am today. His love for me had been complicated, and I hadn't always understood him, but in the end I had turned out fine—in fact, better than fine. Every single dream my father had for me has come true.

As I held my father's hand, and my life with him flashed through my mind, I thought about the question I had often asked myself: If I had known what life with my father would be like, would I have still followed him to El Otro Lado?

You made me who I am, I thought as he took his last breath, and I knew then that the answer to my question was yes.

ACKNOWLEDGMENTS

I have many people to thank for this book! First, I want to thank my editor at Aladdin, Alyson Heller, for believing in my story, and for helping me put it into the hands of young readers to encourage and inspire them to pursue their own dreams. My agent, Adriana Dominguez at Full Circle Literary, for her invaluable guidance and friendship. My editors who worked on the original manuscript—Malaika Adero and Johanna Castillo. I am very lucky to have such a great team at both Atria and Aladdin.

Cory Rayala, my wonderful, supportive husband, who provides a stable and safe home in which I can thrive as writer, mother, and wife. My siblings—Mago, Carlos, and Betty—for helping to fill the gaps of my memory with your own. This book is yours as much as it is mine.

To my father, Natalio Grande, for teaching me to become independent, hardworking, and best of all—a big dreamer. Thank you for teaching me to take advantage of all the opportunities life sends my way.

To Diana Savas, my mentor, my teacher, my friend, my hero.

And finally I thank you, my dear reader, for coming along on this journey with me.

I am deeply grateful to you all.